Contents

national
STATISTICS

FOCUS ON Social Inequalities

2004 edition

Editors Penny Babb, Jean Martin and Paul Haezewindt

Office for National Statistics

London: TSO

Contact points

For enquiries about this publication, contact the Editor:
Penny Babb
Tel: 020 7533 6122
E-mail: penny.babb@ons.gsi.gov.uk

For general enquiries, contact the National Statistics Customer Contact Centre on:
0845 601 3034
(minicom: 01633 812399)
E-mail: info@statistics.gsi.gov.uk
Fax: 01633 652747
Post: Room 1015, Government Buildings, Cardiff Road, Newport NP10 8XG

You can also find National Statistics on the Internet at: **www.statistics.gov.uk**

About the Office for National Statistics

The Office for National Statistics (ONS) is the government agency responsible for compiling, analysing and disseminating many of the United Kingdom's economic, social and demographic statistics, including the retail prices index, trade figures and labour market data, as well as the periodic census of the population and health statistics. It is also the agency that administers the statutory registration of births, marriages and deaths in England and Wales. The Director of ONS is also the National Statistician and the Registrar General for England and Wales.

A National Statistics publication

National Statistics are produced to high professional standards set out in the National Statistics Code of Practice. They undergo regular quality assurance reviews to ensure that they meet customer needs. They are produced free from any political influence.

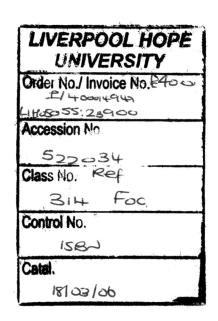

List of Figures and Tables

Page

Page

List of Contributors

Authors: Jean Martin

Paul Haezewindt

Margaret Shaw

Jenny Church

Valerie Christian

Melissa Coulthard

Yuan Huang Chow

Nirupa Dattani

Chris White

Allan Baker

Brian Johnson

Elizabeth Whiting

Production Team: Caroline Hall

Claire Hood

Kirsty Burns

Review Team: Lisa Almqvist

Figen Deviren

Giulio Flore

Caroline Lakin

Kylie Lovell

Trish McOrmond

Acknowledgements

The editors wish to thank all their colleagues in the Office for National Statistics (ONS) who have helped in the preparation of this report. Special thanks go to our colleagues in the ONS Social Analysis and Reporting Division and past and present members of the Socio-Economic Inequalities Branch for their invaluable support in the production of this report.

We have received valuable advice from our independent referees: John Bynner (Institute of Education); John Hills and Abigail McKnight (London School of Economics); Patrick Seyd (University of Sheffield); and Mary Shaw (University of Bristol).

We are grateful also to our colleagues from the following Departments and devolved administrations: Department for Culture, Media and Sport; Department for Education and Skills; Department of Health; Department for Trade and Industry; Department for Transport; Department for Work and Pensions; HM Treasury; Home Office; Inland Revenue; Office of the Deputy Prime Minister; Social Exclusion Unit (ODPM); National Assembly for Wales; Northern Ireland Statistics and Research Agency; Scottish Executive.

Introduction

Jean Martin

Chapter 1

Introduction

Focus On Social Inequalities is part of the Focus On series of publications which combines data from the 2001 Census and other sources to illustrate its topic and provide links to other information. Other reports in the *Focus On* series include analyses of gender, people and migration, ethnicity and identity, religion, health, the labour market, older people, children and young people, families, housing, and Wales: its people. *Focus On* reports comprise of a short overview of the topic area, followed up with more comprehensive analysis in fuller reports, both of which are available from the National Statistics website: *www.statistics.gov.uk/focuson. Focus on Social Inequalities* is the first of the full reports to be published.

This is the second in a series of reports on Social Inequalities. The first was published in 2000.[1] Both reports have been produced in response to increasing numbers of requests for statistics about inequalities, poverty, deprivation and social exclusion. Like the earlier report, it is aimed at a general audience, presenting analyses that are easy to interpret and digest. It includes clearly presented charts and tables and easily understood text. It will provide a resource for all those with an interest in social inequality and related themes, including policy makers, researchers, students and members of the general public.

The report provides an accessible introduction and reference describing issues and trends in present day UK society. It brings together statistics in a number of broad topics areas. In such a wide field it is impossible to be comprehensive; we have had to make choices about what to include. We provide up to date information on various aspects of inequality, building on information presented in the earlier report on education, income, living standards and work, but also covering some new themes: inequalities in health and social participation.

The report draws on a variety of sources and presents time series and historical data where possible to provide a context to show the extent to which a particular aspect of inequality is increasing or decreasing. We look at the advantaged as well as the disadvantaged and explore differences between them. Although we focus on the UK, we include some international comparisons and details for different parts of the UK when relevant comparable information is available. We have taken care throughout to define clearly the concepts used, and to provide references to other data sources or publications which might supplement this report. We hope *Focus on Social Inequalities* is accessible to a wide audience. We welcome feedback and suggestions for future reports. [Email: *inequalities@ons.gov.uk*]

Key concepts

Since 1997 a number of specific policies and government initiatives have been introduced to address disadvantages in health, income, education, community safety and other aspects of welfare and well being. In particular the target was set for eliminating child poverty in a generation. There has therefore been great interest in definitions and measures used to monitor progress towards targets. Terms such as inequality, poverty, social exclusion, deprivation and disadvantage are widely used. There is an extensive literature on all these concepts; here we highlight some of the key features since there are some important differences between them.[1–5]

The term *inequality* refers to disparity or variability between different groups while *inequity* carries an additional implication of injustice or unfairness. Although inequality can be examined in relation to many different areas of life, it is sometimes taken to refer only to income. There are different ways in which inequality can be measured, depending in part on whether the issue of interest is distributed throughout the population (eg income) or is a discrete characteristic such as unemployment. Thus inequalities in income are generally examined by looking at the distribution of income across the population, for example, comparing the income levels of the top and bottom ten per cent of the income distribution. We can also calculate measures of the level of inequality shown by the distribution as a whole. However, we cannot examine unemployment in this way since an individual is either unemployed or not unemployed; there is no comparable unemployment distribution. We can note the proportion of the population that is unemployed but inequalities in unemployment generally refer to differences in unemployment rates between different social groups, for example, between men and women or between different ethnic groups. Health inequalities are typically examined in a similar way, for example, by comparing various health outcomes between different social classes.

Poverty and related concepts such as *social exclusion* and *deprivation* differ from inequality in that they relate only to the bottom end of the distribution or to characteristics of less advantaged social groups. The terms *'poor'*, *'socially excluded'* and *'deprived'* are applied to those who fall below a defined *threshold level*. In general in affluent developed countries like the UK we are concerned less with absolute poverty defined in terms of a lack of the basic necessities for subsistence (such as food, clean water, sanitation, shelter, health) than with relative definitions – about those who are excluded from participation in normal activities in society because they lack the necessary resources. Poverty, social exclusion and deprivation are defined and measured in different ways and also differ in how threshold levels are defined.

Thresholds can be *absolute*; for example poverty can be defined as having an income below a defined monetary value (after allowing for household size and composition) or lacking defined basic necessities, or *relative*, for example, having an income below half or below 60 per cent of the median income. A *relative* threshold will change as the distribution changes, as explained in more detail in the chapter on income inequalities. An absolute threshold does not change in this way but needs to be adjusted regularly as the characteristics of society and what is considered to be necessary for participation in society change over time. However, all thresholds reflect choices about where they should be set rather than real divisions into two categories such as 'poor' and 'not poor'. They are, however, very useful for monitoring purposes in relation to specific targets. Statistics about numbers or proportions of the population above and below thresholds are valuable indicators of the state of society and allow progress over time to be examined.

Social exclusion is described by the Social Exclusion Unit as 'a shorthand for what can happen when individuals or areas face a combination of linked problems such as unemployment, discrimination, poor skills, low incomes, poor housing, high crime, bad health and family breakdown'.[6] It is thus clearly a multi-faceted concept which requires many different measures.

The Government has a number of specific targets in different areas and is monitoring progress towards their achievement. This entails having agreed measures for each target. So, for example, in order to measure progress towards the target of eliminating child poverty in a generation, a precise definition of poverty and how it is to be measured is needed, and the time period to which the target relates must be specified.

It is important to distinguish between inequality on the one hand and concepts which relate to being above or below a defined standard or threshold on the other, since changes can take place in one without necessarily affecting the other.

Inequality is about relative differences. If all groups improve equally (or the whole distribution changes to the same extent), inequality remains the same. Inequality reduces if the most advantaged group moves nearer to the least advantaged or if the least advantaged moves nearer to the most advantaged.

The following diagrams (see Figure 1.1), which show changes over time, illustrate these possibilities. The top line in each shows the position of the most advantaged group as it changes over time and the lower line, that of the most disadvantaged group. The dashed line shows a notional 'poverty threshold'. For simplicity a fixed rather than a relative threshold is shown.

The first diagram (chart a) shows a steady state. The top and

Figure **1.1**

Inequalities: relationship between advantage and disadvantage

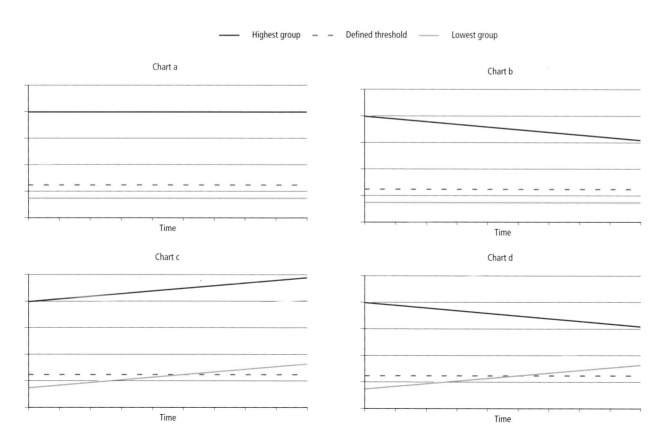

bottom lines are parallel, indicating no change in inequality. The bottom line is not changing relative to the poverty threshold so the proportion of people below this level remains the same.

The next diagram (chart b) shows a decrease in inequality over time, as the top line moves towards the bottom line. But the proportions in poverty have not changed as the bottom line is still the same distance below the threshold.

The third diagram (chart c) shows the bottom line moving upwards, indicating a reduction in poverty. It finishes above the threshold showing that the lowest group is no longer below the poverty threshold. However, the top line shows the same rate of increase – the lines are still parallel – so inequality remains the same.

The final diagram (chart d) shows both a reduction in inequality, as the lines are converging, and in the proportions below the threshold, with the lower line sloping up and eventually crossing the threshold line.

Influences and inter-relationships

This report aims to describe the extent of inequality in a number of key areas of life: education, work, income, living standards, health, and social and civic participation. Wherever possible, we show how these have been changing over time and aim to highlight some of the main inter-relationships between the different areas. For example, while education affects all the other outcomes and educational attainment is of interest as an outcome in its own right, health can affect ability to work which in turn affects income and living standards. Income, education and health all affect social participation and so on.

Within each broad area we have selected which inequalities to describe. We have chosen those which are generally considered to be important and for which reliable data are available. Where possible we aim to go beyond describing inequalities to examine some of the factors which are determinants of inequality. This leads us to consider whether, when talking about inequality, we are most concerned with equality of opportunity or equality of outcome.

Current government policy aims to provide *equal opportunities* between members of social groups defined in terms of fundamental characteristics with which individuals are either born (gender, ethnicity) or over which they have no direct control (eg disability, whether from birth or acquired later in life) and from different types of area. There are policies which aim to reduce inequalities in outcomes between such groups in a number of respects such as educational attainment, employment opportunities, health outcomes and negative characteristics of areas such as high crime and lack of

amenities. However, providing equal opportunities does not necessarily lead to increased equality of outcomes as there are many other influences with many complex and interacting effects on outcomes. There is also growing recognition of the web of complex social, economic and cultural influences which determine relative advantage and disadvantage, many of which are not amenable to influences of public policy. Individuals' life chances are affected initially by such factors as their parents' characteristics – their education, social class and income, all of which can change over time but in general are fairly stable aspects of upbringing. As they grow up and become adult, individuals are subject to many influences and gradually acquire their own educational and social characteristics which may be different from those of their parents. These in turn interact and affect later outcomes over a lifetime.

It can therefore be helpful to think in terms of a life course approach to the study of the determinants of inequality. Individuals are born at a particular point in time with certain characteristics such as gender and ethnic origin. They might also have a disadvantage at birth such as low birthweight or disability. As they develop, they are shaped by influences from a number of sources: their immediate family and household, contact with extended family and other social groups, the housing and area in which they live, access to services (eg health, education) and of course by the process of maturation and moving through different life stages as they get older. Each of these interact and are potential influences on development. We have therefore used a life-course framework in thinking about inequalities (Figure 1.2).

Figure **1.2**

Life-course framework

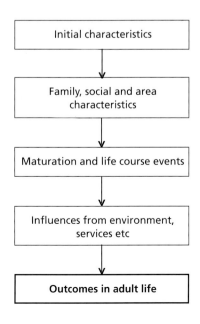

Figure **1.3**

Potential influences upon inequalities

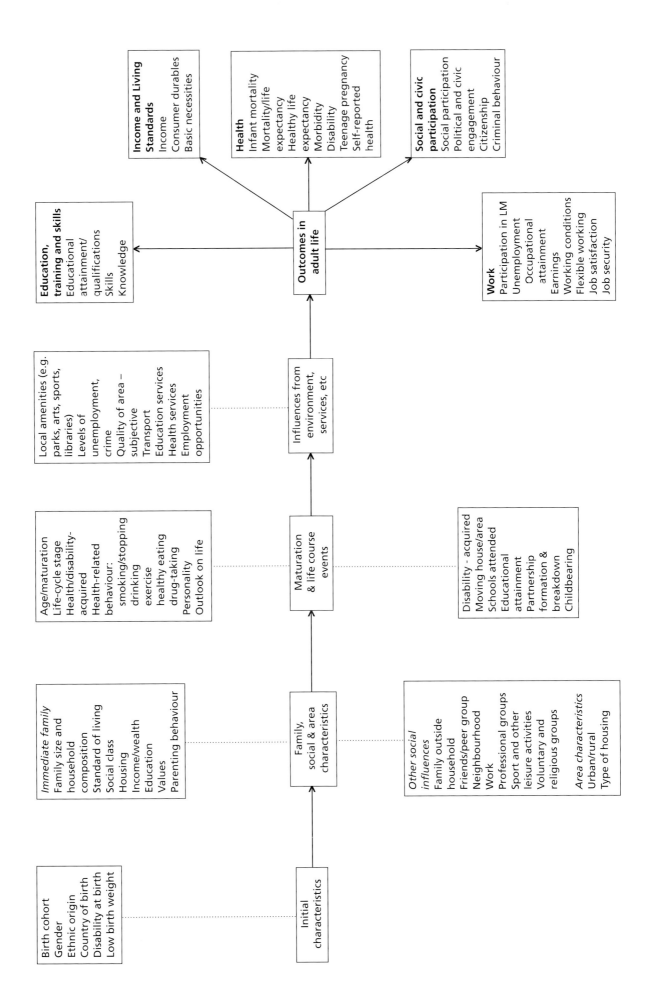

Of course, the relationships are more complex than this simple diagram implies. In Figure 1.3 we list some of the potential influences on inequality in each of these categories but do not attempt to be comprehensive.

Contents and structure of the report

The report is organised into a number of chapters, each concerned with a particular aspect of inequalities: 2: Education, training and skills; 3: Work; 4: Income; 5: Living standards; 6: Health; 7: Participation.

Chapter 2 (*Education, training and skills*) presents analyses at all stages of learning, from pre-school education and compulsory education to further and higher education, adult learning and job-related training. Differences in attainment and participation in education by factors such as social class, income and ethnicity are described. Education is a key determinant for other areas of inequality. Differences in highest qualifications are discussed in relation to their implications for issues such as income, labour market participation, health and social participation.

Chapter 3 (*Work*) focuses on the extent to which different groups of people participate in the labour market and the working conditions, including hours and pay, those in employment experience. The chapter highlights in particular the labour market experiences of people from disadvantaged groups such as lone parents, minority ethnic groups, people with no or lower qualifications, those aged over 50, and those living in the most deprived areas.

Chapter 4 (*Income*) presents analyses of the distribution and sources of income. It focuses particularly on those with low incomes and discusses how people's income can change over time. Also in this chapter is a discussion of wealth, savings and debt and how different sections of the population are affected by these issues.

Chapter 5 (*Living standards*) investigates inequalities in terms of living standards which describe people's living conditions and material circumstances. Factors such as people's access to material resources, decent housing, the quality of the local environment (including incidence of anti-social behaviour and crime), and access to transport and services are discussed.

Chapter 6 (*Health*) examines variations in health linked to people's social and demographic circumstances and geographical location. The chapter explores health inequalities from birth, through childhood to adulthood, health-related behaviour (such as smoking and drinking) and use of health services and how they relate to life expectancy and mortality.

Chapter 7 (*Participation*) presents analyses of people's participation in a range of social and civic activities, and social contact with friends, family and neighbours. Various forms of participation are an important part of social inclusion. The chapter highlights the extent to which different groups participate in society in social organisations, civic activities, volunteering and their contact with social networks and access to social support. Barriers to participation, such as time, cost and access to transport, are also discussed.

References

1. Drever F, Fisher K, Brown J and Clark J (2000) *Social inequalities 2000 edition*. The Stationery Office.

2. Drever F and Whitehead M (1997) *Health inequalities*. Decennial supplement DS No.15. The Stationery Office.

3. Palmer G, North J, Carr J and Kenway P (2003) *Monitoring poverty and social exclusion*. Joseph Rowntree Foundation.

4. McKay A (2002) *Defining and measuring inequality*. Inequality Briefing Papers no. 1. Department for International Development.

5. *Opportunity for all* (2004) Sixth annual report. Department for Work and Pensions.

6. Social Exclusion Unit (2004) *Breaking the cycle. Taking stock of progress and priorities for the future*. Office of the Deputy Prime Minister, page 3.

Education, Training and Skills

Paul Haezewindt

Chapter 2

Introduction

Education, training and the acquisition of skills are crucial for people to progress and prosper in society. Education is considered both a cause and consequence of inequality and is strongly related to issues such as poverty and social exclusion. Having few or no qualifications and lacking basic skills can have negative social and economic outcomes in terms of employment, income, living standards, health and social participation.

People from disadvantaged backgrounds often perform less well at school and gain fewer qualifications than those from more advantaged backgrounds. Advantage or disadvantage can be passed down through generations, where people's educational attainment is frequently related to that of their parents. Education can however provide a route out of poverty and social exclusion. Those with the best qualifications and skills are more likely to progress in society, irrespective of their background.

Early years

Effective learning in the early years of life is strongly associated with immediate and lasting social and educational benefits for all children. Development in children as young as 22 months is a strong predictor of educational qualifications at age 26 years.[1] Attending pre-school or nursery education classes prior to starting compulsory education at age 4 or 5 enhances children's development compared with those who do not attend. Research by the Effective Provision of Pre-school Education (EPPE) Project in England found that average scores in school entry assessments of cognitive and social development (such as letter recognition and verbal comprehension) were higher among children that had attended pre-school, compared with those that had not attended.[2]

Low parental socio-economic status, low household income and low parental education levels are strongly related to a child's poor intellectual skills at entry to pre-school. Nursery education does not eliminate differences caused by social backgrounds but does improve child development over and above family influences and therefore helps to combat social exclusion for those from disadvantaged backgrounds.[2]

An early start to nursery education is related to better intellectual development, improved independence, concentration and sociability, helps children assimilate better into primary school and increases a child's receptivity for learning.[2] The main nursery education providers are nursery schools, reception classes, day nursery and play group/pre-schools. Through the Government's Sure Start programme, all three and four year olds are entitled to a free part-time early

years place. Sure Start provides a range of early education, childcare, health and family support services, and Sure Start local programmes provide community-based services in the most disadvantaged areas.

An annual survey in 2002 for the Department for Education and Skills (DfES) of parents of three and four year old children in England found that 96 per cent of children had attended nursery education in the past week.[3] Participation had risen steadily since 1997 when 92 per cent of children had participated.

While overall high proportions of three and four year olds had participated in nursery education, there were variations in the rates of participation between certain groups. Participation rates were found to increase with the age of the child. In 2002, 87 per cent of younger three year olds had participated in nursery education in the past week compared with 100 per cent of older four year olds.

Participation rates also differed by family circumstances such as social class (see Appendix, Part 2: Socio-economic classification), family composition, working status and income. Children with parents in professional or managerial occupations were more likely to participate in nursery education, and to participate at an earlier age, than children from other social class backgrounds. Children from two-parent families were more likely to attend nursery education than those from lone-parent families. For both types of families, participation rates were highest among the children of working parents. Participation rates increased with household income, ranging from 93 per cent participation for children from households with an annual income of less than £10,000, to 98 per cent of children from households with an annual income of £30,000 or more. The participation rates of younger children in particular differed by household income. Seventy seven per cent of younger three year olds from households with annual incomes of less than £10,000 attended nursery education, compared with 95 per cent for those from households with annual incomes of £30,000 or more.

In 2002 only three per cent of parents of three and four year old children in England had not used any nursery education or childcare in the past year. The main reason given by parents for not using early years services, around three out of ten, was that the parent preferred to look after the child themselves (Table 2.1). However, many parents who were not able to send their child/children to a nursery education or childcare provider cited a lack of adequate provision as the cause. Almost a quarter of parents stated that there was a lack of space at local providers and a tenth stated that there were no local providers. For a fifth, cost was a barrier to access.

As well as nursery activities, learning with the family at home is also considered important. Research by the EPPE Project indicated that the quality of the learning environment at home had a significant influence upon child development. Home learning activities such as reading to children, teaching nursery rhymes, playing with friends, teaching the alphabet and visiting the library were associated with better intellectual and social development. The EPPE study found that the home learning environment was only moderately associated with factors such as social class and parental education levels, and what parents did with their children had a more important impact than their own background or circumstances.

Compulsory education

Education is compulsory for all children between the ages of 5 (4 in Northern Ireland) and 16. The National Curriculum is divided into four defined key stages (see Appendix, Part 2: National curriculum). At ages 7, 11 and 14 (Key Stages 1, 2 and 3) pupils are assessed formally by national tests and teacher assessments of the core subjects: English, Mathematics and Science. Key Stage 4 of the National Curriculum is the final stage of compulsory education for pupils in the United Kingdom, and at around age 16, most pupils are assessed by public examination. In England, Wales and Northern Ireland the main examination taken is the General Certificate of Secondary Education (GCSE). In Scotland the equivalent examination

taken is the Scottish Certificate of Education: Standard Grade (SCE (S)). These examinations can be taken in a wide range of subjects and have an important impact upon future opportunities in further education/training and employment.

Key Stages 1–3

Table 2.2 shows the proportion of pupils in England in 2003 reaching or exceeding expected standards in tests in English, Maths and Science at Key Stages 1 to 3, and teacher assessments in Information Communication Technology (ICT) at Key Stage 3. There was little difference in attainment levels between girls and boys for Maths and Science at any of the key stages. However, large differences in attainment levels by sex were found for writing, English and ICT. The gap in attainment level in writing was 17 percentage points higher for girls than boys at Key Stage 2. Similarly there was a difference in English of 10 percentage points at Key Stage 2 and was 14 percentage points higher at Key Stage 3. Teacher assessments at Key Stage 3 recorded the proportion of girls achieving or exceeding

Table 2.1

Reasons for non-participation[1] in nursery[2] education, 2002

England	Percentages
Reasons not able to use nursery education	
Local providers full/could not get a place	24
Child too young for local provider	23
Too expensive/cost factors	18
No local providers	9
Child dislikes/unhappy in nursery education	5
Reasons did not want nursery education	
Prefer to look after child at home	29
Parent prefers to teach child him/herself	12
Child not yet developed enough to benefit	4
Other	14

1 More than one response could be given. Non-participation in the last year.
2 Nursery education providers: nursery schools, nursery class, reception class, day nursery and play group/pre-school and childcare.

Source: National Centre for Social Research for the Department for Education and Skills

Table 2.2

Pupils reaching or exceeding expected standards: by key stage, sex and subject[1], 2003

England		Percentages
	Boys	Girls
Key Stage 1[2]		
Reading	80	88
Writing	76	87
Mathematics	89	91
Key Stage 2[3]		
English	70	80
Reading	78	84
Writing	52	69
Mathematics	73	72
Science	86	87
Key Stage 3[4]		
English	61	75
Reading	61	74
Writing	59	72
Mathematics	69	72
Science	68	68
ICT[5]	63	71

1 Assessment by task or test.
2 About age 7, proportion achieving level 2 or above.
3 About age 11, proportion achieving level 4 or above.
4 About age 14, proportion achieving level 5 or above.
5 Teacher assessment.

Source: Department for Education and Skills

expected standards in ICT at 71 per cent compared with 63 per cent of boys.

Research by the DfES highlights that pupil performance at Key Stages 1 to 3 and at GCSE level (or equivalent) also differs by pupil ethnicity, whether English is a first language or not, incidence of Special Educational Needs (SEN), and eligibility for Free School Meals (FSM).[4] FSM eligibility is used as an indicator of low household income, deprivation and social class. Pupils are eligible for FSM if their family receives Income Support or income-based Jobseekers Allowance. In 2003, pupils in England from Chinese and Indian groups consistently achieved above the national average across each Key Stage and at GCSE level. Black African, Black Caribbean, Bangladeshi and Pakistani pupils, however, performed consistently below the national average for each Key Stage and at GCSE level. For all Key Stages and at GCSE level, pupils with English as their first language performed better than pupils with English as an additional language; and pupils with no SEN performed better than pupils with SEN. Pupils not eligible for FSM performed better than those who were eligible in each Key Stage and at GCSE level.

Pupil progression

Pupils progress through the school system at different rates. Pupil progression differs from pupil attainment as it describes how pupils improve in relation to their previous levels of attainment. The 2002 *Pupil Progress by Pupil Characteristics* report by the DfES highlighted the rates of progress for particular groups of pupils through school from Key Stages 1 to 4 (GCSE level) in England. Some of the key findings are described below.[5]

Pupils not eligible for FSM progressed more than those who were eligible from each prior attainment level in each subject at every Key Stage. All pupils, whether entitled to FSM or not, made better progress in schools with lower proportions of pupils eligible for FSM than schools with higher proportions of pupils eligible for FSM. Generally, pupils with English as an additional language progressed more than those with English as their first language – which may party be explained by these pupils progressing more at school as they become more proficient in English. Also, some of the higher achieving minority ethnic pupils may have English as an additional language.

Indian, Chinese and Bangladeshi pupils tended to make above average progress throughout school. Among boys, Chinese pupils progressed most at all Key Stages. For girls, Pakistani pupils began as one of the poorest progressing groups at Key Stage 2, but by Key Stage 4 (GCSE level) were one of the best

progressing groups. Black Caribbean pupils, both male and female, and both those eligible for FSM or not, made below average progress at all Key Stages.

GCSE attainment

The attainment of five or more GCSEs at grades A* to C (equivalent to O Level qualifications taken prior to the introduction of GCSEs in 1986, with the first examinations being taken in 1988) is considered a benchmark of attainment. The Government has made a commitment to increase the proportion of those aged 16 achieving five GCSEs at grade A* to C (or equivalent) by two per cent each year on average between 2002 and 2006, and in all schools for at least 20 per cent of pupils to achieve this standard by 2004 rising to 25 per cent by 2006. Overall, the proportion of pupils in England gaining five or more higher grade (A* to C) GCSEs has increased steadily over the last decade. In 2002/03, 53 per cent of pupils gained five or more higher grade GCSEs compared with 41 per cent in 1992/93. In Wales the proportion of pupils achieving this level of attainment increased from 36 per cent in 1992/93 to 51 per cent in 2002/03. Attainment in Northern Ireland also increased from 48 per cent to 59 per cent over the same period and equivalent attainment levels in Scotland increased from 48 to 58 per cent. The levels of attainment have increased in recent years for most groups of pupils; however, differences in attainment levels between different groups have also increased.

Parental and family circumstances, such as household income, socio-economic group, parental qualifications and parental support, all impact upon attainment. Differences in attainment at GCSE level can also be found by factors such as pupil ethnic group, sex, and by the type of school attended.

Figure 2.3 compares FSM eligibility and GCSE attainment, or equivalent, by local education authorities (LEA) in the United Kingdom. In 2001/02, LEAs with low proportions of pupils eligible for FSM generally had higher proportions of pupils gaining five or more higher grade GCSEs than LEAs that had high proportions of pupils eligible for FSM. For LEAs with between 0 and 10 per cent of pupils eligible for FSM, 57 per cent of pupils gained five or more higher grade GCSEs. LEAs with greater than 30 per cent of pupils eligible for FSM recorded 41 per cent of pupils gaining five or more higher grade GCSEs.

The proportion of pupils eligible for FSM varies considerably by ethnic group. According to the Pupil Level Annual School Census (PLASC) in 2003 all ethnic groups in England (with the exception of Indian (12 per cent) and Chinese (11 per cent) pupils) had a higher proportion of primary and secondary

Figure **2.3**

Attainment of five or more GCSE grades A* to C[1]: by free school meal eligibility in local education authorities[2], 2001/02

United Kingdom

Percentages

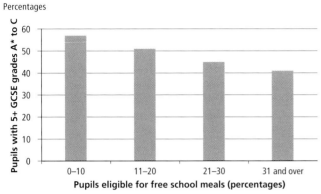

1   Scottish Certificate of Education (SCE)/Standard Grade/National Qualifications (NQ) in Scotland.
2   Local education authorities in England and Wales. Local authorities in Scotland. Education and library boards in Northern Ireland.

Source: Department for Education and Skills; National Assembly for Wales; Scottish Executive; Northern Ireland Department of Education

school pupils eligible for FSM than the majority White British school population (14 per cent). Particularly high pupil eligibility of FSMs could be found among Bangladeshi (50 per cent), Black African (42 per cent) and Pakistani (35 per cent) pupils.

A report by OFSTED in 2000 on ethnicity and GCSE attainment found that for each of the main minority ethnic groups in England there was at least one LEA where each of these groups was the highest attaining.[6] In general, however, certain ethnic groups tend to gain a greater proportion of higher grade GCSEs than others. Data from the DfES for England in 2003 show that Chinese pupils were the most likely to achieve five or more GCSE grades A*-C: 79 per cent of the girls and 71 per cent of the boys (Figure 2.4). Indian pupils had the next highest achievement levels: 70 per cent and 60 per cent of Indian girls and boys respectively achieved these levels. White pupils were the third best performing group, with girls achieving 57 per cent of A*-C grades, compared with 46 per cent of the boys. The lowest levels of GCSE attainment were among Black Caribbean pupils. Only 25 per cent of these boys and 40 per cent of the girls achieved five or more A*-C grade GCSEs. Pupils from the Other Black, Black African and Pakistani groups had the next lowest levels of attainment.

The attainment levels of pupils from all ethnic groups has improved over time. Some ethnic groups, however, have improved much more than others. Bangladeshi pupils, one of the lowest performing ethnic groups over the last decade, have shown the largest improvements in terms of the proportion of pupils gaining five or more higher grade GCSEs. This

Figure **2.4**

Pupils achieving five or more GCSEs grades A* to C/ GNVQs: by ethnic group and sex, 2003

England

Percentages

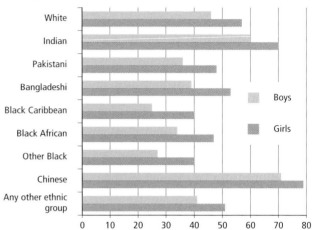

Source: National Pupil Database, Department for Education and Skills

proportion increased by 27 percentage points from 14 per cent in 1992 to 41 per cent in 2002 (Figure 2.5). Black pupils showed the least improvement, with an increase of 13 percentage points from 1992 to 2002.

In 2002 girls in England and Wales continued to outperform boys in terms of gaining higher grade GCSEs, as has been the case over the last decade. Fifty six per cent of female pupils gained five or more higher grade GCSEs in 2002, compared with 46 per cent of male pupils; a gap of 10 percentage points. The gap in attainment level has increased gradually over time. In 1992, 40 per cent of female pupils achieved five or more higher grade GCSEs compared with 33 per cent of male pupils; a gap of seven percentage points.

Figure **2.5**

Attainment of five or more GCSE grades A* to C: by ethnic group[1], 1992 to 2002

England & Wales

Percentages

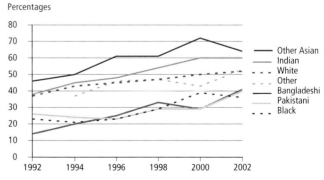

1   Data for the Other ethnic group in 1992 are not available due to small sample size. The Other Asian ethnic group includes the Chinese group.

Source: Youth Cohort Study, Department for Education and Skills

Some of the largest inequalities in the attainment of GCSEs can be found between pupils of parents belonging to different socio-economic groups (Figure 2.6). In 2002, 77 per cent of children with parents in higher professional occupations in England and Wales gained five or more higher grade GCSEs, more than double the proportion of children with parents in routine occupations (32 per cent).

Figure **2.6**

Attainment of five or more GCSE grades A* to C: by parental NS-SEC, 2002

England & Wales

Percentages

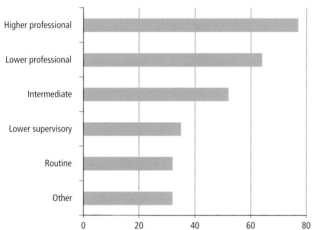

Source: Youth Cohort Study, Department for Education and Skills

The gap in GCSE attainment levels by parental socio-economic group has increased over time (see Appendix, Part 2: Socio-economic status). In 1992, 60 per cent of children with parents in 'managerial/professional' occupations (broadly equivalent to NS-SEC higher professionals) attained five or more higher grade GCSEs, compared with 16 per cent of children with parents in 'unskilled manual' occupations (broadly equivalent to NS-SEC routine occupations); a gap of 44 percentage points (Table 2.7).

In 1998 this gap rose to 49 percentage points its highest point in the last decade.

Pupils with highly educated parents tended to achieve higher grades than children with less well educated parents. In 2002, 71 per cent of pupils in England and Wales with at least one parent with a degree level qualification achieved five or more higher grade GCSEs. The same level of attainment was obtained by 60 per cent of pupils who had at least one parent with an A level qualification, and by 40 per cent of pupils where neither parent had an A level qualification (Figure 2.8). A recent research report by the DfES outlined the importance of parental support in maximising pupil's potential from schooling.[7] Parental involvement is strongly related to achievement. Parental involvement can take many forms, and is characterised by such activities as good parenting in the home, engagement with the school and intellectual stimulation of the child.

The National Adult Learning Survey (NALS) in 2002 found that parents in England and Wales with no qualifications were more than three times less likely to have done any learning activities in the past 12 months with their child (aged 8 to 18) than parents with higher degrees. Those with household incomes lower than £10,399 were over six times less likely to do learning activities with their child than parents with a household income of more than £31,200. Differences in the extent and form of parental involvement are also associated with family social class, parental health and single parent status.

Other pupils that were less likely than the general school population to gain higher grade GCSEs include pupils with a statement of special educational needs (SEN), children in care and those with a disability or health problem. Only five per cent of pupils in England with a statement of SEN in 2002

Table **2.7**

Attainment of five or more GCSE grades A* to C: by social class/NS-SEC[1], 1992 to 2002

England & Wales Percentages

Social class	1992	1998	NS-SEC	2000	2002
Managerial/Professional	60	69	Higher professional	74	77
Other non-manual	51	60	Lower professional	61	64
Skilled manual	29	40	Intermediate	45	52
Semi-skilled manual	23	32	Lower supervisory	35	35
Unskilled manual	16	20	Routine	26	32
Other	18	24	Other	24	32

1 Social class from 1992 to 1998, and NS-SEC from 2000 to 2002.

Source: Youth Cohort Study, Department for Education and Skills

Figure **2.8**

Attainment of five or more GCSE grades A* to C: by highest parental qualification, 2002

England & Wales
Percentages

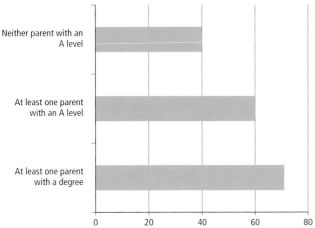

Source: Youth Cohort Study, Department for Education and Skills

Figure **2.9**

Attainment of five or more GCSE grades A* to C[1]: by school type[2], 2002/03

England
Percentages

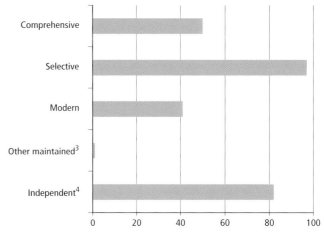

1   Or GNVQ equivalent.
2   For definition of school types see Appendix, Part 2: School types.
3   Including community and foundation special schools, hospital schools and pupil referral units.
4   Including non-maintained special schools.

Source: Department for Education and Skills

OECD PISA study

gained five or more higher grade GCSEs compared with 58 per cent of pupils with no identified SEN.[4] In 2001/02 eight per cent of children in England who had spent at least one year in care gained five or more higher grade GCSEs compared with half of all other children.[8] For pupils in England and Wales with a disability or health problem in 2002, 36 per cent gained five or more higher grade GCSEs, compared with 52 per cent of those without a disability or health problem.[9]

The type of school that pupils attended highlights differences in the likelihood of gaining qualifications (see Appendix, Part 2: School types). In 2002/03 those attending a selective school in England were almost twice as likely to gain five or more higher grade GCSEs as those attending a comprehensive school (Figure 2.9). In selective schools 97 per cent of pupils gained five or more higher grade GCSEs compared with 50 per cent of those from comprehensive schools. Only one per cent of those at special community and foundation schools, hospital schools and pupil referral units obtained five or more higher grade GCSEs. However, only seven per cent of pupils at these schools were entered for five or more GCSE examinations, compared with 91 per cent of pupils in all schools. For those attending an independent school, 82 per cent gained five or more higher grade GCSEs. The backgrounds and abilities of pupils at different types of school can vary considerably. Research by the DfES into the value added by schools (i.e. pupil progress compared with initial ability) found that the type of school attended had little impact upon how individual pupils progressed.[10]

Research by the Organisation for Economic Co-operation and Development (OECD), found that the United Kingdom ranked among the best performing countries in terms of the literacy skills of 15 year olds in reading, mathematics and science.[11] The Programme for International Student Assessment (PISA) conducted by the OECD in 2000 measured the skills and knowledge of 15 year olds across 32 countries. Among EU countries taking part in the PISA assessments, the United Kingdom ranked second for mathematics and science, and third for reading, all well above the OECD average (Table 2.10 - see overleaf).

In comparison to other OECD countries the United Kingdom was found to be a low equity as well as a high attainment country. The socio-economic background of students in the United Kingdom had a higher than average impact upon student performance compared with other countries in the study. For example, students from disadvantaged backgrounds in the United Kingdom were more than twice as likely as other students in the United Kingdom to be among the poorest performing (lowest 25 per cent) in reading literacy tests. The characteristics associated with low achievement in the PISA study in England included being male, from a lower socio-economic background, having parents with lower or no qualifications, living in a single parent household, having many siblings, attending a state rather than independent school, and attending a school with a high rate of FSM eligibility.[12]

Table **2.10**

Knowledge and skills of 15 year olds in three literacy areas[1]: EU comparison[2], 2000

Mean scores

	Reading	Mathematics	Science
Finland	546	536	538
Irish Republic	527	503	513
United Kingdom	**523**	**529**	**532**
Sweden	516	510	512
Austria	507	515	519
Belgium	507	520	496
France	505	517	500
Denmark	497	514	481
Spain	493	476	491
Italy	487	457	478
Germany	484	490	487
Greece	474	447	461
Portugal	470	454	459
Luxembourg	441	446	443
OECD average	500	500	500

1   *Programme for International Student Assessment. See Appendix, Part 2: OECD PISA study.*
2   *The response rate of schools in the Netherlands was too low to allow accurate estimates of literacy.*

Source: Organisation for Economic Co-operation and Development

Non-attendance at school

Truancy

The DfES estimates that over 50,000 pupils a day miss school without permission in England, and 7.5 million school days are missed each year through truancy. Common characteristics among truants are that they tend to be older pupils, from poorer backgrounds, have parents that are in low skilled jobs, and live in local authority housing. High levels of truancy are also found among Traveller children (mostly of Gypsy, Roma or Irish heritage).

The Social Exclusion Unit cites poor parental supervision and a lack of parental commitment to education as a key cause of truancy, as well as the influence of friends and peers, and school-based factors such as bullying or anxiety about coursework.[13] A truancy survey conducted by the DfES across English LEAs in December 2002 found that 50 per cent of pupils found truanting from school were accompanied by a parent or adult. Other research indicates that 44 per cent of truants believed their parents knew that they were truanting, while 48 per cent of non-truants were held back from missing school by the fear of their parents finding out.[14]

Exclusions

Permanent exclusions in England rose sharply in the 1990s. In 1990/91, 2,910 pupils were excluded. This figure increased fourfold to a peak of 12,668 in 1996/97. In recent years the number of exclusions declined to 8,323 in 1999/2000 but has since increased to 9,540 in 2001/02. This figure is small in relation to the overall school population, representing 0.12 per cent of all pupils. However, being excluded from school has a big impact upon the excluded child and also affects the wider community.

The majority of pupils excluded were White teenage boys. In 2001/02, 82 per cent of pupils permanently excluded from school in England were boys, 82 per cent were White and 78 per cent were aged between 12 and 15. However, children from certain ethnic groups were particularly likely to be excluded (Figure 2.11). In 2002/03 the highest rate per head of population of permanent exclusions in England was found among Black Caribbean pupils at 37 per 10,000, over three times the rate of White pupils excluded (12 per 10,000) and twenty times the rate for Chinese pupils (2 per 10,000), who were the least likely group to be excluded. The rate of exclusions for Black Caribbean pupils has, however, declined sharply since 1997/98 (76 per 10,000), while rates of exclusions for other ethnic groups have remained fairly stable. Children with SEN and those in care were also more likely to be excluded than the school population as a whole. Pupils with statements of SEN in England in 2002/03 were nine times more likely to be excluded than those with no SEN. In 2001 children in care in England were ten times more likely to be excluded compared with those not in care.[8] Exclusion rates vary

Figure **2.11**

Permanent exclusions[1]: by ethnic group, 2002/03

England
Rate per 10,000 pupils

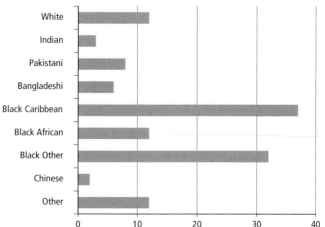

1   *Permanent exclusions of pupils of compulsory school age.*

Source: Department for Education and Skills

considerably from school to school. A large proportion of all exclusions are concentrated in a small number of schools and rates tend to be highest in areas of high social deprivation.

As well as truancy and exclusion, children can have poor attendance records for many other reasons. Other groups of children likely to have poor attendance records include pupils caring for a sick or disabled relative, children from families under stress, pregnant school girls and young/teenage mothers, and Traveller children. The benefits and opportunities which education can bring, particularly for those from disadvantaged backgrounds, cannot be gained if children do not attend school regularly. Absence from school through truancy and exclusion has a serious impact upon the likelihood of gaining qualifications. In 2002 pupils in England and Wales who were persistent truants in year 11 were over four and a half times less likely to gain five or more higher grade GCSEs than those who did not truant from school. A quarter of persistent truants gained no qualifications compared with two per cent of non-truants (Figure 2.12). Permanently excluded pupils or those excluded for a fixed term were almost three times less likely to gain five or more higher grade GCSEs than those not excluded from school. Thirteen per cent of excluded pupils gained no qualifications compared with three per cent of non-excluded pupils.

Poor attendance at school also has social and economic consequences for those missing school and the wider community. Those who miss school are more likely than pupils that regularly attend school to not continue full-time education after compulsory schooling ends and be out of work at age 18. Missing school is also linked to crime and homelessness. An Audit Commission survey of young offenders found that 42 per cent had been excluded from school and 23 per cent had truanted significantly.[15] Home Office research also found that male truants were almost five times more likely to offend than male non-truants and female truants were almost eight times more likely to offend than female non-truants.[16]

Post compulsory education

At age 16 compulsory education ends. Continuing education and participating in further and higher education to study for and obtain higher qualifications is shown to have a range of positive social and economic benefits. Benefits include improved employment chances and earning potential, as well as benefits for health, well being and social participation. Lifelong learning through adult learning or job-related training can also help to improve people's career prospects and gives adults with low or no qualifications a chance to improve their basic skills.

Further Education (FE)

The majority of 16 year olds continue their education in some way. In 2002, 87 per cent of 16 year olds in England were in

Figure **2.12**

Academic attainment[1]: by truancy and exclusion[2], 2002

England & Wales

Percentages

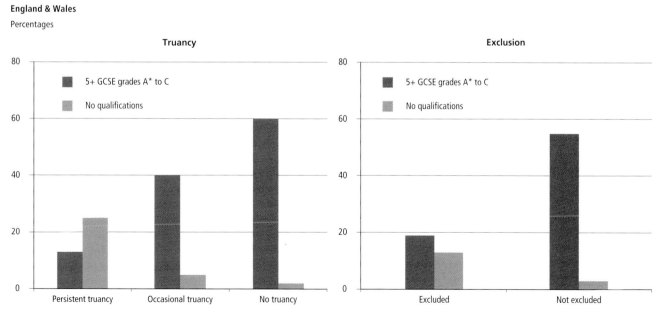

1 GCSE and GNVQ qualifications in year 11.
2 Truancy in year 11, excluded fixed term or permanently in years 10 or 11.

Source: Youth Cohort Study, Department for Education and Skills

education or training. Seventy three per cent were in full-time education, seven per cent in work-based learning, three per cent in employer-funded training and four per cent in other training (such as part-time education, or in training in independent institutions). The pattern was similar in Wales with 72 per cent of 16 year olds in full-time education, eight per cent in government training schemes and a further seven per cent in part-time education.

According to the YCS, young people with parents from higher socio-economic backgrounds were more likely to continue their full-time education at age 16 than those from lower socio-economic backgrounds. In 2002, 87 per cent of those with parents in higher professional occupations in England and Wales participated in full-time education, compared with 58 per cent of those with parents from lower supervisory occupations and 60 per cent of those with parents in routine occupations. However, differences in participation rates between students from different socio-economic backgrounds decreased significantly once prior attainment levels were taken into account. People with the best qualifications from school were most likely to continue their education irrespective of social background.

In 2002, those in England and Wales with the best GCSE results were almost three times more likely to be in full-time education at age 16 than those with the poorest results. Ninety four per cent of those with eight or more higher grade GCSEs were in full-time education at age 16, compared with 32 per cent of those with one to four GCSEs at grades D to G, and 35 per cent of those with no GCSEs (Figure 2.13). The impact of

Figure **2.13**

Continuing full-time education at age 16: by GCSE[1] qualifications, 2002

England & Wales
Percentages

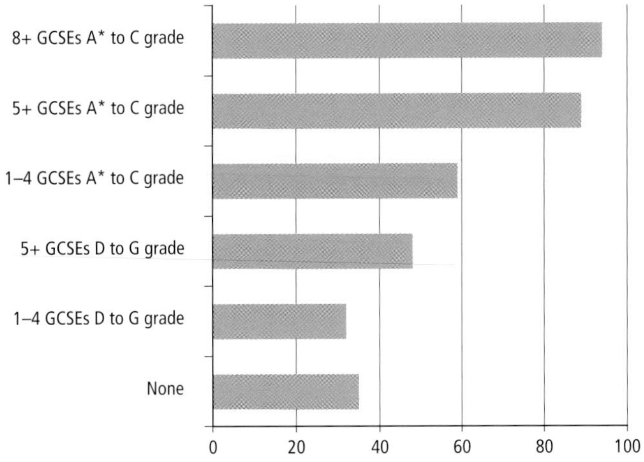

1   Includes equivalent GNVQ qualifications in year 11.

Source: Youth Cohort Study, Department for Education and Skills

prior attainment upon continuing education at age 16 has decreased over the past decade, particularly for those with no qualifications. In 1992, 19 per cent of those with no qualifications continued full-time education at age 16, compared with 35 per cent of those with no qualifications in 2002.

Student characteristics such as ethnic origin and sex also demonstrated notable differences in staying on into full-time education. In 2002 disparities in participation rates by ethnic group in England and Wales ranged from 69 per cent of White 16 year olds, the least likely to participate, to 91 per cent of the Indian group, the most likely to participate. Females aged 16 were more likely than males to continue in full-time education, with 75 per cent of girls compared with 66 per cent of boys participating in full-time education.

Age 18 tends to be another milestone or transitional period in educational development. At this age many of those who stayed in full-time education at age 16 have completed their further education courses and have the choice of continuing their studies or seeking employment. The YCS found that in 2002, 13 per cent of 18 year olds in England and Wales were not in education, employment or training. These included those with no qualifications or fewer/lower grade GCSEs or equivalent, those who had been truant or excluded from school and people with a disability or health problem. According to the DfES, the proportion of young people in education or training in England at age 18 in 2002 was around a third less than those aged 16. By age 18, 60 per cent of people were in education or training compared with 87 per cent at age 16. Thirty seven per cent of 18 year olds were in full-time education, while eight per cent were each in work-based learning and employer-funded training and seven per cent in other education and training. The majority of those in full-time education were in higher education. The participation rate in the United Kingdom at age 18 is particularly low when compared internationally with other OECD countries. In 1999, Turkey and Mexico were the only countries in the OECD group with fewer 18 year olds enrolled in education than the United Kingdom.

Higher education (HE)

Participation in HE in the United Kingdom has increased rapidly over the past thirty years from 460,000 full-time students in 1970/71 to around 1.3 million in 2001/02. HE provides courses that are of a higher standard than qualifications such as A levels, Higher Grades in Scotland, and GNVQ/NVQs at level 3 (see Appendix, Part 2: National vocational qualification levels). There are three main levels of HE course: first degrees; Higher National Diplomas and Diplomas in HE; and higher degrees.

The proportion of young people participating in HE, as measured by the Age Participation Index (API), has increased sevenfold since 1960. The API measures the proportion of young people who enter HE for the first time by the age of 21. In 1960 five per cent of young people in Great Britain participated in HE. By 2001, 35 per cent of young people participated.

Growth in the number of people attending HE institutions was significantly affected by an increase in the number of women entering HE. Thirty years ago many more men entered HE than women, during the 1990s this trend reversed. Women comprised just under a third of those in HE (both full- and part-time) in 1970/71. By 2001/02 there were over a fifth more women than men in HE.

There has always been a significant gap in HE participation between those from different social class backgrounds. In recent years this gap has increased (Figure 2.14). In 2001, 50 per cent of young people from non-manual backgrounds (those from professional, managerial and intermediate occupations) participated in HE compared with 19 per cent of young people from manual social class backgrounds (those from skilled manual, semi-skilled manual and unskilled manual occupations), a gap of 31 percentage points. In 1960 the gap in participation rates between those from non-manual and manual backgrounds was 23 percentage points.

Table **2.14**

Higher education participation[1]: by parental social class, 1960 to 2001

Great Britain   Percentages

	1960	1970	1980	1990	1995	2001
Non-manual[2]	27	32	33	37	47	50
Manual[3]	4	5	7	10	17	19
Total participation	5	8	12	19	32	35

1 Participation by Age Participation Index (API): proportion of young people who enter HE for first time by age 21.
2 Non-manual social class group includes professional, managerial and technical and skilled non-manual occupations.
3 Manual social class group includes skilled manual, semi-skilled manual and unskilled manual occupations.

Source: Department for Education and Skills

Prior attainment is the main cause of the difference in participation rates in HE between those from different social class backgrounds. The social class gap in HE participation disappears to a great extent once prior attainment is taken into account. As Figure 2.15 shows, those from higher or lower social class backgrounds are almost equally as likely to enter HE if they have the same A level results. Larger differences can be

Figure **2.15**

Entry into higher education by age 21: by socio-economic group (SEG) and highest qualification[1] at age 18, 2002

England & Wales

Percentages

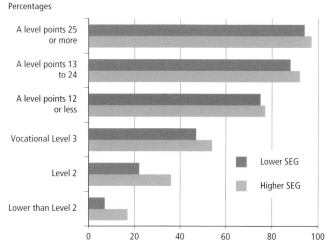

1 For an explanation of A level points system, see Appendix, Part 2: GCE A level points score system.

Source: Youth Cohort Study, Department for Education and Skills

found for those with lower academic or vocational qualifications. Twice the proportion of people from higher rather than lower social class backgrounds with a qualification lower than NVQ level 2 entered HE by age 21. In 2002 those in England and Wales with a highest qualification of NVQ level 3 or above (broadly equivalent to 2 A levels) at age 18 were five times more likely than those with a NVQ level 2 qualification (equivalent to 5 A* to C grade GCSEs) to be in full-time HE, and twenty six times more likely than those with below a NVQ level 2 qualification.

Young people's social class background has an influence upon what type of university they go to. The 2003 DfES report *Widening participation in higher education*, highlighted that people from manual socio-economic backgrounds with the appropriate qualifications were less likely to attend an elite university, such as a Russell Group university, than those from a non-manual background.[17] Russell Group universities are made up of nineteen of the older, more established universities, and are heavily over subscribed in terms of applications. The report indicates that application rates to Russell Group universities were significantly lower from applicants from manual socio-economic backgrounds compared with those from non-manual backgrounds. The acceptance rates from these universities were found to be similar for both groups. This suggests that application rates are the main cause of differential access to these universities for people from different socio-economic backgrounds. The same results were shown in terms of educational background, where those from state schools were less likely to apply to an elite university than those from an independent school. Also, few minority ethnic students attend elite universities. Minority ethnic students tend to be concentrated in a relatively small number of HE institutions, mainly in modern (post 1992) universities in London and other large cities, located close to their parental home.[18]

Lifelong learning

Many adults continue their education, to improve knowledge about a subject, for enjoyment, or to develop new skills, often with a view to improve their prospects in the labour market. Adult learning activities include taught courses and self-directed learning such as on the job training and other forms of professional development. Adult learning activities cover a multitude of vocational and non-vocational subjects, and take place in a wide range of settings including the home, schools, community centres, and the work place.

The National Adult Learning survey found that a high proportion of people in England and Wales were engaged in learning activities. In 2002, 76 per cent of adults aged 16 to 69, who were outside of full-time continuous education, had taken part in learning activities in the previous three years, an increase of two percentage points from 1997. Despite the overall high proportion of people involved in learning activities, participation rates were low among certain groups. Particularly low rates of participation were found among older adults, aged 60 to 69 (51 per cent). Those with no qualifications (29 per cent) or basic skills difficulties (52 per cent) were also less likely

to participate in learning than the general population, as were people on low incomes (55 per cent), those with work-limiting disabilities (56 per cent) and those living in deprived areas (67 per cent, compared with 88 per cent in the least deprived areas).

The main reasons given by non-learners for not taking part in learning activities were a lack of interest in learning, or that they preferred to spend time doing other things (Table 2.16). A lack of time was often cited as a barrier due to looking after a family, work commitments and childcare responsibilities. Other obstacles for non-learners included not knowing about local learning opportunities, being nervous about returning to the classroom (24 per cent) and having difficulties paying course fees.

Data from the Labour Force Survey showed that in spring 2003 around a sixth of working age people in the United Kingdom in paid employment had received some form of job-related training in the previous four weeks. Young men aged 16 to 19 were most likely to have received job-related training, followed by women aged between 20 and 24. The rates of job-related training declined with age for both men and women, with those aged 45 to retirement age less likely to have received training. For adults aged 20 and above, women were more likely to have received job-related training than men.

Those with highest qualifications in the workplace were more likely to receive job-related training than those with lower or no qualifications (Figure 2.17). People with the highest

Table **2.16**

Reasons[1] for not learning given by non-learners, 2002

England & Wales   Percentages[2]

Prefer to spend time doing other things	*38*
Not interested in learning	*29*
Lack of time due to family	*27*
Does not know about local learning opportunities	*26*
Nervous about going back to classroom	*24*
Lack of time due to work	*23*
Hard to pay course fees	*22*
Too old to learn	*21*
Do not have qualifications to get on to course	*21*
Lack of time due to children	*18*
Worried about keeping up with course	*18*

1 *Selected responses; all responses shown which applied to 18 per cent or more of respondents.*
2 *Percentages do not sum to 100 per cent as respondents could give more than one reason.*

Source: National Adult Learning Survey, Department for Education and Skills

Figure **2.17**

Employees[1] receiving job-related training[2]: by highest qualification[3] and sex, spring 2003

United Kingdom
Percentages

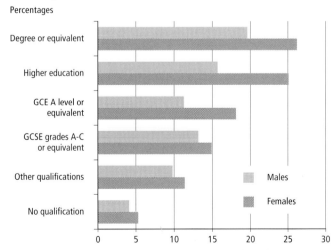

1 *Males aged 16 to 64, females aged 16 to 59 in paid employment.*
2 *Job-related training in the last 4 weeks.*
3 *Excludes those who did not know their highest qualification level.*

Source: Labour Force Survey, Office for National Statistics

qualifications were therefore more likely to gain more work-related skills and experiences, aiding their job/career prospects, compared with those with low or no qualifications. Men and women with degrees were approximately five times more likely to have received job-related training in the past four weeks than those with no qualifications.

Skills, qualifications and outcomes

Basic skills

A minimum requirement of education and learning is to acquire a range of basic skills that help people to function and progress in society. Basic skills include the ability to read, write, speak English/Welsh, and use mathematics. Proficiency with ICT is regarded as a further basic skill. In 2002/03 the DfES commissioned a Skills for Life survey that examined the basic skills of adults aged 16 to 65 in England. It measured literacy, numeracy and ICT skills, and performance was grouped over broad levels of competence based upon a framework of national standards for adult basic skills (see Appendix, Part 2: Skills for life national standards framework). The survey found that a high proportion of adults in England had poor basic skills in literacy and an even greater proportion had poor basic skills in numeracy: 16 per cent had literacy skills below the standard of a D to G grade GCSE (Entry Level or below) and 47 per cent had numeracy skills at this level (Table 2.18). People with good literacy skills tended to have good numeracy skills, and those with poor literacy skills tended to have poor numeracy skills.

Characteristics of adults with low literacy and numeracy skills included people from minority ethnic groups and also those

Table **2.18**

Adult[1] basic skill levels, 2002/03

England   Percentages

| | Literacy | Numeracy | Information communication technology (ICT) | |
			Awareness	Practical
Entry level or below (lowest skill level)[2]	16	47	25	53
Level 1[3]	40	28	25	38
Level 2 or above (highest skill level)[4]	44	25	50	9

1 Adults aged 16 to 65.
2 Below the standard of a D to G grade GCSE.
3 Equivalent to GCSE grade D to G. ICT practical skills are at Level 1 and above.
4 Equivalent to GCSE grade A* to C.

Source: Skills for Life Survey, Department for Education and Skills

with English as an additional language. Low skills were also found among those living in deprived areas, people from lower socio-economic groups, older adults (aged 55 to 65), and those with poor health. Women had similar literacy skills compared with men, but were more likely to have lower numeracy skills.

In terms of ICT skills, the survey measured both people's awareness of ICT and terminology, and their practical skills in the use of ICT applications. Many people were found to have high levels of skills in both awareness and the practical use of ICT. Fifty per cent achieved the highest skill level, equivalent to GCSE grades A* to C (Level 2) or above in awareness skills, and 38 per cent achieved the second highest skill level (Level 1) in practical assessments, equivalent to GCSE grade D to G and above. A further 9 per cent achieved level 2 or above. However, a significant proportion of people had poor ICT skills. A quarter of adults had an awareness of ICT equivalent or below the standard of GCSE grades D to G (Entry Level or below), and just over half of adults (53 per cent) had practical skills at this level, including 15 per cent of adults that had never used a computer.

Raising the skill levels of working adults is a key Government target. The Government has stated an aim to reduce by at least 40 per cent the number of adults in the UK workforce who lack NVQ level 2 or equivalent qualifications by 2010 (from a baseline in 1998). Adults in the labour market without such qualifications are entitled to have access to free learning, and support is offered through Jobcentre Plus, New Deal programmes and Work Based Learning for Adults. The proportion of working age adults in England without a NVQ level 2 or higher qualification has fallen from 39 per cent in 1998 to 34 per cent in 2003.

Highest qualifications

Qualifications are the formal recognition of learning and the acquisition of particular skills at a certain level. Qualifications are of particular importance in finding employment. Sixteen per cent of the working age population in the United Kingdom in spring 2003 were educated to degree level, 68 per cent had other qualifications and 15 per cent had no qualifications. Across the United Kingdom there were considerable variations in qualification levels. Table 2.19 (see overleaf) shows the highest qualifications held by people in the countries of the United Kingdom and the government office regions within England. The proportion with a degree varied from 24 per cent in London to 11 per cent in the North East. Northern Ireland had the highest proportion of people with no qualifications (24 per cent), while the South East and South West had the lowest proportion with 11 per cent.

Table **2.19**

Highest qualification[1,2]: by region, spring 2003

United Kingdom

Percentages

	Degree or equivalent	Other qualifications	No qualification
United Kingdom	16	68	15
North East	11	70	19
North West	13	69	18
Yorkshire and Humberside	13	70	16
East Midlands	13	69	17
West Midlands	13	69	18
Eastern	16	70	14
London	24	62	14
South East	20	69	11
South West	16	73	11
Wales	15	68	17
Scotland	15	70	15
Northern Ireland	13	63	24

1   Excludes those who did not know their highest qualification level.
2   Males aged 16 to 64, females aged 16 to 59. Figures may not sum due to rounding.

Source: Labour Force Survey, Office for National Statistics

Qualification levels vary considerably by age. Results from the Labour Force Survey in spring 2003 showed that the proportion of adults in the United Kingdom with a degree peaked at 25 per cent for men and 23 per cent for women between the ages of 25 and 34. The proportion with a degree then declined with increasing age to 14 per cent of men and eight per cent of women aged between 55 and the respective retirement ages. The proportion of those with no qualifications also increased with age. Men aged between 55 and 64 were more than twice as likely to have no qualifications than those aged 25 to 34. For women, those aged 55 to 59 were three times more likely to have no qualifications than those aged between 25 and 34.

The higher attainment of qualifications among younger, compared with older adults, is largely a product of changing society and education systems. The growth in HE participation over the last forty years generally, and particularly for women, has resulted in higher rates of degree level qualifications among later generations. Figure 2.20 shows the proportion of people in Great Britain (aged in their early 30s) from different birth cohorts with a first or higher degree. The proportion with a degree increased from 21 per cent of men and 10 per cent of

women in 1978 to 31 per cent of men and 32 per cent of women in 2000. Similarly, a drop in the proportion of people with no qualifications occurred in later birth cohorts. Forty five per cent of men and women aged 32 in 1978 had no qualifications compared with 13 per cent of men and 14 per cent of women aged 30 in 2000.

Large differences in qualification levels can be found between ethnic groups. Among men in Great Britain, Black Caribbeans and Bangladeshis were the least likely to have a degree (nine and 11 per cent respectively) in 2002/03. In contrast, more than twice the proportion of degrees occurred among Chinese (28 per cent), Indian (27 per cent) and Black African and White Irish (23 per cent each) men - the groups with highest proportions of degrees. Among women, the Bangladeshi and Pakistani groups were the least likely to have a degree (four per cent and nine per cent respectively). Chinese women were the most likely to have a degree (25 per cent), followed by White Irish women (23 per cent), and those in the White Other and Indian groups (20 per cent each).

Figure **2.20**

Attainment of first or higher degrees for birth cohorts[1] aged in their early 30s: by sex

Great Britain

Percentages

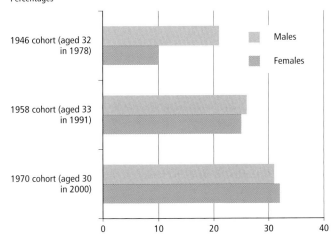

1   For an explanation of British birth cohort surveys see Appendix, Part 2: British birth cohort studies.

Source: British Cohort Study, National Child Development Study and National Study of Health and Development

Figure 2.21 shows the proportion of people with no qualifications by ethnic group. Particularly high proportions of people with no qualifications occurred among the Bangladeshis (at 46 per cent for women and 38 per cent for men) and Pakistanis (36 per cent and 29 per cent for women and men respectively). For the other ethnic groups the proportions with no qualifications were mostly between 15 and 20 per cent for both men and women. The differences were generally small

Figure **2.21**

No qualifications[1]: by ethnic group[2] and sex, 2002/03

Great Britain

Percentages

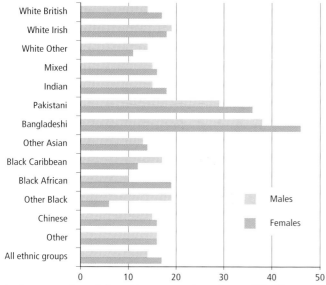

1 As a proportion of all working age people: males aged 16–64, females aged 16–59.
2 The number of respondents for males and females in the Other Black ethnic group is very small. The same applies for the males in the Chinese ethnic group. Therefore the figures for these groups are only indicative.

Source: Annual Local Area Labour Force Survey, Office for National Statistics

between the sexes; however, large gender differences occurred in the Pakistani, Bangladeshi, Black African and Other Black groups. It is important to note that differences in the age structure of different ethnic populations have not been taken into account. The 2001 Census highlighted that people from minority ethnic groups tended to be younger than the White population. Mixed, Pakistani, Bangladeshi, Other Black and Black African groups had particularly high proportions of under 16s and fewer over 65s.

Among minority ethnic groups, age is closely related to country of birth – those aged under 35 years are more likely than their peers to have been born inside the United Kingdom. Qualifications for ethnic groups can vary considerably for people born in or outside of the United Kingdom. In general, those born inside the United Kingdom are more likely to have qualifications than their peers born outside the United Kingdom. For example, Black Africans were much more likely to have a degree if they were born in the United Kingdom (a difference of 21 percentage points). Similarly, Bangladeshis, Pakistanis, Indians and Black Caribbeans, were particularly more likely to have no qualifications if they were born outside of the United Kingdom (31, 23, 16 and 16 percentage points difference respectively). However, the pattern was not true for all groups. Among people from the Mixed ethnic groups, those

born outside of the United Kingdom were much more likely than those born inside the United Kingdom to have a degree (a difference of 10 percentage points).

Effects of education on key areas of life

There are persuasive incentives for people to raise their levels of education. Education has both direct and indirect consequences for a range of positive and negative social and economic outcomes that are explored elsewhere in this publication, and include issues such as labour market participation, earnings, social participation, health, well being and crime.

Having qualifications, and in particular higher qualifications, has a significant impact upon the likelihood of gaining employment. In spring 2003 the difference in employment rates for those with no qualifications compared with those with any qualifications was at least 21 percentage points, and increased with highest level of qualification up to degree level. Eighty eight per cent of working-age people in the United Kingdom with a degree were in employment compared with 50 per cent of those with no qualifications (Figure 2.22 - see overleaf). Rates of employment differ little between those whose highest qualifications were GCSEs or A levels. In contrast employment was 10 percentage points higher for those with a degree level qualification compared to those with A levels. Having higher qualifications also has a major impact upon the level of earnings people can expect. People with a degree, earned on average, gross weekly earnings of £632 in full-time employment, compared with £298 for those with no qualifications. There is a clear relationship between higher qualifications and higher earnings, and the earnings premium for possessing a degree is particularly high.

People with low basic skills and lower or no qualifications exhibit lower levels of public involvement. Results from the 2001 British Household Panel Survey suggested that people in Great Britain with higher qualifications were more likely to join in the activities of a range of social, cultural, community and political organisations than those with lower or no qualifications. Sixty per cent of those with a degree regularly participated in organisations compared with 48 per cent of those with other qualifications and 37 per cent of those with no qualifications. Results from the Home Office Citizenship Survey in 2001 also found that those with higher qualifications were more likely to participate socially in groups, clubs and organisations (Table 2.23 - see overleaf). The survey suggested that those with higher qualifications were more likely to be civically engaged and volunteer both formally and informally than those with lower or no qualifications.

Figure **2.22**

Employment rate and gross weekly earnings[1]: by highest qualification[2], spring 2003

United Kingdom

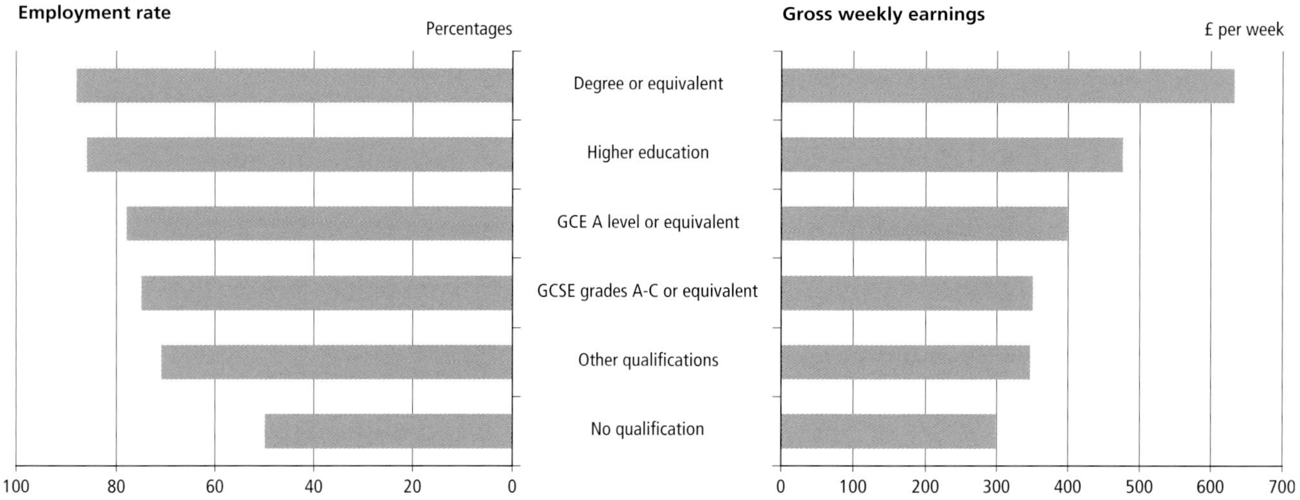

Employment rate	Gross weekly earnings

1 Males aged 16 to 64, females aged 16 to 59. Full-time employees only based upon respondents self assessment. Respondents who did not report an hourly wage or who reported hourly pay greater than £100 are excluded.
2 Excludes those who did not know their highest qualification level.

Source: Labour Force Survey, Office for National Statistics

According to the 2001 Census, people aged 16 to 74 in the United Kingdom with a first or higher degree were much more likely to report being in good health than those with no qualifications – a difference of between 19 and 24 percentage points for both sexes (age standardised to take account of the differences in the age structure of the two groups). The highest proportion of self-reported health was for men with a degree in Northern Ireland at 81 per cent, compared with 60 per cent for men with no qualifications living in the same area. The equivalent figures in England and Wales and Scotland were 78–79 per cent for men with a degree and 58–59 per cent for men with no qualification. The proportions of self-reported

good health by qualification were consistently higher in Northern Ireland than in Scotland or England and Wales, although the differences were generally small. The exception was for women with a first or higher degree who showed a difference of six percentage points: 78 per cent in Northern Ireland compared with 75 per cent in Scotland and 72 per cent in England and Wales. The comparable figures were between 52 and 54 per cent for women with no qualifications. For all groups, the proportions for women were consistently lower than for men (a difference of between three and six percentage points).

Table **2.23**

Social and civic participation[1]: by highest qualification[2], 2001

England & Wales

Percentages

	Social participation	Civic participation	Informal volunteering	Formal volunteering
Degree or above[3]	82	53	79	57
Other qualification	69	39	71	41
No qualifications	48	28	52	23
All	65	38	67	39

1 See Appendix, Part 2: Social and civic participation.
2 Adults aged 16 and above.
3 Includes first degree, higher degree and postgraduate qualifications.

Source: Citizenship Survey, Home Office

Research indicates that the extent and involvement of young people (aged 12 to 30) in committing crime is among other factors, influenced by a poor experience of school, including disaffection from school, low achievement, truancy and exclusion. Results from the Youth Lifestyles Survey in 1998/99 showed that in England and Wales, men aged between 17 and 30 with no qualifications were nearly three times as likely to commit a serious offence (29 per cent) as those with some qualifications (11 per cent). For women, the rates of offending were also found to be higher among those with no qualifications (eight per cent) compared with those with qualifications (three per cent).

Conclusion

The level of educational achievement is a key factor in the difference between advantaged and disadvantaged groups in areas such as employment, income, health and living standards. Socio-economic gaps in education begin early and can widen through the education system. Participation and attainment in education can vary considerably by family and individual characteristics such as social class, household income, ethnicity, having English as an additional language, incidence of special educational needs, health problems and disability. Parents' own experiences of education, qualifications gained and commitment to learning also have a significant impact upon their children's progress and achievement at school. However, people from all socio-economic backgrounds can gain valuable skills and qualifications. Prior attainment is a key factor in determining how people achieve at school and their participation and progress in further or higher education. Therefore, inequalities and underachievement in all stages of schooling, from pre-school and beyond, are important to understand and address in order to reduce educational inequalities and consequently other aspects of social inequalities.

References

1. Feinstein L (2003) Inequality in the early cognitive development of British children in the 1970 cohort, *Economica*, 70, 73–97

2. Effective Provision of Pre-School Education Project, *http://www.ioe.ac.uk/cdl/eppe/index.htm*

3. Bell A and Finch S (2004) Sixth Survey of parents of three and four year old children and their use of early years services, National Centre for Social Research, Department for Education and Skills, RR 525, *http://www.dfes.gov.uk/research/data/uploadfiles/RR525.pdf*

4. Department for Education and Skills (2004) National Curriculum Assessments and GCSE/GNVQ attainment by pupil characteristics, in England, 2002 (final) and 2003 (provisional), SFR 04/2004, *http://www.dfes.gov.uk/rsgateway/DB/SFR/s000448/NPD_sfr_text_Finished3.pdf*

5. Department for Education and Skills (2003) Statistics of Education: Pupil progress by Pupil Characteristics: 2002, *http://www.dfes.gov.uk/rsgateway/DB/SBU/b000402/pupil_progress_final.pdf*

6. Gillborn D and Safia Mirza H (2000) Educational Inequality: mapping race, class and gender, OFSTED, HMI 232, *http://www.ofsted.gov.uk/publications/index.cfm?fuseaction=pubs.displayfile&id=447&type=pdf*

7. Desforges C and Aboucharr A (2003) The impact of parental involvement, parental support and family education on pupil achievements and adjustments: a literature review, Department for Education and Skills, RR 443, *http://www.basic-skills-observatory.co.uk/uploads/doc_uploads/702.pdf*

8. Social Exclusion Unit (2003) A Better Education for Children in Care, Social Exclusion Unit Report, *http://www.socialexclusion.gov.uk/downloaddoc.asp?id=32*

9. Department for Education and Skills (2003) Youth Cohort Study: The Activities and Experiences of 16 Year Olds: England and Wales 2002, SFR 04/2003, *http://www.dfes.gov.uk/rsgateway/DB/SFR/s000382/V4sfr04-2003.pdf*

10. Department for Education and Skills (2003) National Curriculum Assessments for Key Stage 2 (revised) and Key Stage 1 to Key Stage 2 Value Added Measures for 11 Year Olds in England for 2002/03 (revised), SFR 33/2003, *http://www.dfes.gov.uk/rsgateway/DB/SFR/s000433/sfr332003.pdf*

10. Organisation for Economic Co-operation and Development (2002) *Education at a Glance*, OECD Indicators 2002.

11. Gill B, Dunn M and Goddard E (2002) Student achievement in England, Results in reading, mathematical and scientific literacy among 15-year-olds from OECD PISA 2000 study, Office for National Statistics, London: The Stationary Office, *http://www.statistics.gov.uk/downloads/theme_education/PISA_2000.pdf*

12. Social Exclusion Unit (1998) Truancy and Social Exclusion - Report by the Social Exclusion Unit, *http://www.socialexclusion.gov.uk/downloaddoc.asp?id=239*

13. O'Keeffe (1993) Truancy in English Secondary Schools (cited in reference 12).

14. Audit Commission (1996) Misspent Youth (cited in reference 12)

15. Flood-Page C, Campbell S, Harrington V and Miller J (2000) Youth crime: Findings from the 1998/99 Youth Lifestyles Survey, Home Office Research Study 209, Home Office: London, *http://www.homeoffice.gov.uk/rds/pdfs/ hors209.pdf*

16. Department for Education and Skills (2003) Widening participation in higher education, *http://www.dfes.gov.uk/ hegateway/hereform/index.cfm*

17. Bhattacharyya G, Ison L and Blair M (2003) Minority Ethnic Attainment and Participation in Education and Training: The Evidence, University of Birmingham and Department for Education and Skills, RTP01-03, *http://www.basic-skills-observatory.co.uk/uploads/doc_uploads/751.pdf*

Further Reading

Department for Education and Skills (2003) Education and Skills: The Economic Benefit, *http://www.dfes.gov.uk/ economicbenefit/docs/Eco_Social%20Text.pdf*

Fitzgerald R, Taylor R and LaValle I (2003) National Adult Learning Survey (NALS) 2002, National Centre for Social Research, Department for Education and Skills, RR 415, *http://www.dfes.gov.uk/research/data/uploadfiles/ RR415.pdf*

Makepeace G, Dolton P, Woods L, Joshi H and Galinda-Rueda F (2003) From school to the labour market, p29–64, in Ferri E, Bynner J, and Wadsworth, M (eds) (2003) *Changing Britain, Changing Lives*, Institute of Education.

Work

Margaret Shaw

Chapter 3

Introduction

When discussing social inequalities, work is important for many reasons. Earnings from work are a primary source of income for the majority of households and individuals. Income, in turn, influences relative experiences of affluence or poverty. More broadly, however, work can provide networks of friends and colleagues, a sense of participation in society or social inclusion, and opportunities for personal and professional development.

Family life has been altering over recent decades, such that cohabitation before marriage is more frequent and partnership formation is happening later. Marital breakdown has become more common as have lone-parent families and changes in care responsibilities for children and older relatives. The demographic structure of the UK is also changing and people are living longer. Also more young people are entering higher education and remaining in education longer. These factors have all impacted upon how and when people experience work. The labour market itself has undergone significant change in the past few decades. Paid work has changed from a predominance of full-time permanent jobs mostly held by men to a varied mix of full-time and non-standard forms of work. The decline of agriculture and of manufacturing jobs held by men, together with the growth of service jobs taken up by women, has resulted in a very different employment structure at the beginning of the 21st century.

This chapter covers a broad range of labour market issues, highlighting some of the most topical. Trends in employment, unemployment and economic inactivity are discussed. Throughout the chapter, labour market advantage is described principally in terms of those who are employed, and then in terms of the earnings acquired from employment. Disadvantage is discussed mainly in terms of worklessness, but also by focusing on particular groups in the population that have been identified as having significant labour market disadvantage.

Employment

In spring 2003 the UK labour market was buoyant with the numbers of people in work at record levels. The last decade has seen a rise in both full-time and part-time working and generally people are working in more flexible ways. The UK's employment rate is among the highest in Europe and its unemployment rate the lowest.

People are considered to be economically active, or in the labour force, if they are aged 16 or over and are either employed or actively looking for work (see Glossary of terms on page 39). In spring 2003 there were 29.6 million people

who were economically active in the United Kingdom, of whom 28.1 million were in employment, the highest employment level on record. This number has risen from around 25.6 million in spring 1971. The rise in the employment level reflects an increase in the UK population, though there have also been other impacts over the past few decades, for example, the fall in employment in the early 1980s and 1990s. The working-age employment rate is currently being sustained at around 75 per cent. However, as shown in Figure 3.1, over the past few decades there have been quite different trends in male and female employment.

Figure **3.1**

Employment rates[1]: by sex[2]

United Kingdom

Percentages

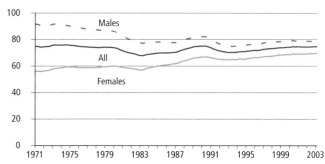

1 Seasonally adjusted. Pre-1992 data are taken from the ONS Experimental LFS-Consistent Time Series. See Appendix, Part 3: LFS Experimental Time Series.
2 Employment rates for working age people: men aged 16 to 64 and women aged 16 to 59.

Source: Labour Force Survey, Office for National Statistics

The male working-age (16 to 64 years) employment rate was over 90 per cent in the early 1970s, but by spring 2003 it was just below 80 per cent. Male employment was already on a downward trend during the 1970s, but it was particularly affected by the two recessions of the early 1980s and 1990s. The more male-dominated industries, such as manufacturing, have tended to be hit harder during the economic slow downs and this shows up in male unemployment data. In comparison, while the female employment figures do show the effect of the economic cycle it is less marked. More generally, female employment has been growing, reflecting changes in society (such as improved educational qualifications and the overall shift towards greater societal acceptance of women with children working) and the switch from manufacturing to services. This shift has opened up more opportunities for women, whether in the type of work or in more flexible working hours. In total, the female working-age (16 to 59 years) employment rate increased from about 56 per cent in 1971 to almost 70 per cent in spring 2003, the highest on record and when women made up 46 per cent of those in employment.

More women now decide to delay marriage and family formation and childcare options have improved. This has a significant bearing on women's employment choices and employment rates do vary significantly according to whether women have dependent children and the age of the children. Forty eight per cent of women with a child aged under two are in employment, compared with 90 per cent of similar men. However, the employment of women with young children has increased – the employment rate of women with a child under five has grown from 42 per cent in 1991 to 54 per cent in 2001.

Despite the overall health of the labour market there are pockets of people who are less engaged and who have not entered or remained in employment. Individuals can have unequal access to job opportunities because of where they live, their age, gender, ethnicity or skill, and quite often because of a combination of these factors. A recognition that certain groups traditionally fare worse than others in the labour market informs the Department for Work and Pensions' (DWP) Public Service Agreement (PSA) target 'to increase the employment rates of disadvantaged areas and groups, taking account of the economic cycle'. The key groups are people with disabilities, lone parents, minority ethnic groups, people aged over 50, those with the lowest qualifications and people living in the 30 UK local authority districts with the poorest initial labour market position. The Government's intention is to reduce the difference between their employment rates and the overall, national rate.[1]

Table 3.2 shows that employment rates have risen through the 1990s for all of the disadvantaged groups except for the group with no formal qualifications, a rapidly shrinking sector of the population. Growth in employment for each of the other groups has, since the late 1990s, generally been greater than the growth in overall employment. Between 1994 and 2003 the employment rate for the over 50s rose from 63 per cent to 70 per cent and for lone parents the increase was from 42 per cent to 53 per cent. Over the same period, the rate for those with the lowest qualifications fell from 54 per cent to 51 per cent.

The UK working-age population is becoming better qualified and, as mentioned above, the proportion of the population with no qualifications has declined sharply from 22 per cent in 1996 to 15 per cent in 2003 (Figure 3.3). Poor or low level qualifications are associated with an increased risk of long-term unemployment and higher levels of qualifications lead to higher levels of employment (see Chapter 2).

Table **3.2**

Employment rates: by disadvantaged groups[1]

United Kingdom			Percentages
	1994	1999	2003
Older people[2]	63	65	70
30 LAs[3]	59	60	64
Minority ethnic groups	51	56	58
Lone parents	42	49	53
Low qualifications[4]	54	50	51
Disabled	..	46	49
All	71	74	75

1 Employment rates for working age people: men aged 16 to 64 and women aged 16 to 59. Figures are not Census adjusted. See Appendix, Part 3: Labour Force Survey data.
2 Those aged 50 to 64 for men and 50 to 59 for women.
3 People living in the 30 local authority districts with the poorest initial labour market position.
4 People with no formal qualifications.

Source: Department for Work and Pensions, HM Treasury from Labour Force Survey

Figure **3.3**

Highest qualification levels: by working age[1] population[2]

United Kingdom

Percentages

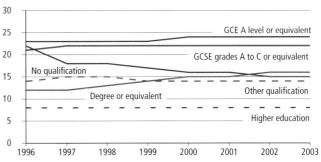

1 Males aged 16 to 64, females aged 16 to 59.
2 Figures are not Census adjusted. See Appendix, Part 3: Labour Force Survey data.

Source: Department for Work and Pensions, HM Treasury from Labour Force Survey

Working patterns

With the rapid growth in employment among women, notably those with children, coupled with employers' concerns relating to competitive pressures, labour shortages and the need to retain employees, has come an increasing recognition of the challenges faced in reconciling work and family life. A significant outcome has been an increased interest in flexible working arrangements such as part-time work, flexi-time, job sharing, homeworking and 'family friendly' policies (including the implementation and extension of statutory maternity rights, parental leave, help with childcare, career breaks and the like). The former can be of benefit to workers with or without children, while the latter are specifically about managing work and childcare. Access to these arrangements is likely to be influenced by a wide range of factors and such arrangements are by no means widely or equally available. Research has highlighted that certain arrangements may only be available to a limited number or narrow range of employees while some forms of flexible working - such as flexible working or homeworking - may be more subject to negotiation than others.[2] There is some evidence that where these schemes are offered, they are most likely to be targeted towards high skill employees. Provision seems to be greater in the public sector and in large private sector companies. Women report greater access than men, though this may be explained by differences in men's and women's experiences of managing work and family responsibilities (and therefore their interest in gathering information about what is available and making use of that provision). The following section looks at actual take-up of the various types of flexible working.

Full-time working is the most common arrangement for both working men (90 per cent) and women (56 per cent) (Table 3.4). However, as outlined above, part-time working is popular with many employees and employers because of the flexibility it offers to combine work with activities such as caring responsibilities and other interests. In spring 2003 a much higher proportion of women than men worked part time, 44 per cent and 10 per cent respectively.

Different reasons are given as to why people take up part-time work (Table 3.5). The overwhelming majority, four out of five women, say they do not want full-time work, double the proportion of men giving this reason. In the last decade there has been an increase in the proportions choosing part-time work because they are in education. Between 1993 and 2003 for men this rose from 28 per cent to 32 per cent of those working part time and for women, from 7 per cent to 12 per cent. Over the same period the proportion saying they could not find a full-time job has fallen from 30 per cent to 16 per cent of men and from 11 per cent to 6 per cent of women.

Table **3.5**

Reasons for part-time employment: by sex

United Kingdom						Percentages
	Males		Females		All	
	1993	2003	1993	2003	1993	2003
Student or at school	28	32	7	12	10	16
Ill or disabled	3	4	1	1	2	2
Could not find full-time job	30	16	11	6	14	8
Did not want full-time job	39	47	81	81	74	74

Source: Labour Force Survey, Office for National Statistics

In spring 2003, five per cent of male employees and seven per cent of female employees were in temporary jobs (Table 3.4). For men the most common reason for being in temporary work was because a permanent job could not be found. Women

Table **3.4**

Full-time, part-time and temporary working[1]: by sex, spring 2003

United Kingdom

	Males		Females		All	
	Thousands	Percentages	Thousands	Percentages	Thousands	Percentages
Total in employment[2]	15,082	100	12,841	100	27,922	100
Employees	12,565	83	11,848	92	24,413	87
Self-employed	2,436	16	901	7	3,337	12
Full-time	13,552	90	7,185	56	20,737	74
Part-time	1,529	10	5,656	44	7,185	26
Temporary employment	667	5	808	7	1,475	6

1 *Employment rates are seasonally adjusted and for all 16 and over.*
2 *Total in employment also includes unpaid family workers and those on government supported training and employment programmes.*

Source: Labour Force Survey, Office for National Statistics

were much more likely to opt for temporary work because they did not want a full-time job.

In spring 2003 just under one in five people in full-time employment and just under one in four part-time employees said they had a flexible working arrangement. Women are much more likely than men to be working in flexible ways (Table 3.6). Flexible working hours is the most commonly cited arrangement for full-time men and women and part-time men. Part-time women are more likely to work in term time with a high proportion being teachers or having other jobs in schools.

Table **3.6**

Employees with flexible working patterns[1], spring 2003

United Kingdom   Percentages

	Males	Females	All employees
Full-time employees			
Flexible working hours	9.1	14.5	10.9
Annualised working hours	4.1	4.7	4.3
Four and a half day week	1.5	1.0	1.4
Term-time working	1.0	5.0	2.4
Nine day fortnight	0.3	0.2	0.3
Any flexible working pattern[2]	16.5	25.7	19.7
Part-time employees			
Flexible working hours	6.3	8.3	7.9
Annualised working hours	2.9	3.7	3.6
Term-time working	3.1	10.1	8.7
Job sharing	0.9	2.6	2.3
Any flexible working pattern[2]	15.4	25.8	23.7

1 Percentages are based on totals that exclude people who did not state whether or not they had a flexible working arrangement. Respondents could give more than one answer.
2 Includes other categories of flexible working not separately identified.
Source: Labour Force Survey, Office for National Statistics

As the employment rate of the UK has risen in recent years, every region of the UK has experienced increased employment. There remain, however, variations in employment rates between regions, and even greater differences within regions (Figure 3.7). Employment rates tend to be considerably lower in cities, though there are some areas with relatively low employment outside of cities; for example, the valleys of South Wales, areas in the North East and some seaside towns. The highest employment rates tend to be in smaller market towns. It is in London where the greatest contrast is found between local authorities. The region contains Tower Hamlets, with the lowest employment rate in the UK (53 per cent), and

Richmond upon Thames, with a rate of 82 per cent. The local authorities with the highest employment rate are Forest Heath in the East and Tandridge in the South East, both with rates of 88 per cent.

Figure **3.7**

Regional employment rates[1] and ranges within regions, 2002–03[2]

United Kingdom

Percentages

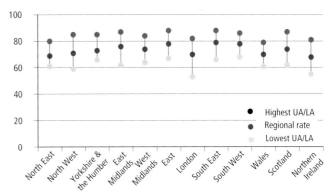

1 Employment rates for working age people: men aged 16 to 64 and women aged 16 to 59.
2 Data are not Census adjusted but are consistent with population estimates published in February 2003.

Source: Annual Local Area Labour Force Survey, Office for National Statistics; Northern Ireland Statistics and Research Agency

Earnings

Earnings from work are a primary source of income for the majority of households and individuals. As shown in Table 3.8 (see overleaf) for the 2002/03 tax year, the average weekly gross earnings for full-time adults whose pay was not affected by absence stood at £476, an increase of 2.6 per cent since April 2002. Part-time weekly earnings rose more quickly to stand at £152. Men's full-time earnings increased by 2.1 per cent in the year to April 2003, compared with a higher growth in women's earnings of 3.7 per cent. Women's weekly earnings were lower than men's partly because they worked on average 3.5 fewer hours per week. In spring 2003 the largest difference was in London, where women's pay was 76 per cent of men's and the smallest gap was in Wales, at 88 per cent.

Although average hourly pay provides a useful comparison between the earnings of men and women, it does not necessarily indicate differences in rates of pay for comparable jobs. Pay averages in part are affected by the different work patterns of men and women, such as the proportions in different occupations and their length of time in jobs. Women are over-represented in low-income groups and have lower employment rates than men. They are particularly likely to have low incomes at key stages of their life cycle. For example, both lone mothers and single older women are more likely to have

Table **3.8**

Average gross weekly earnings: by employment status and sex

Great Britain

£ per week / percentage

	2002			2003			Percentage change		
	Men	Women	All	Men	Women	All	Men	Women	All
Adults whose pay was unaffected by absence									
Full-time	514	382	464	525	396	476	2.1	3.7	2.6
Part-time	165	144	148	164	150	152	−0.6	4.2	2.7
All	484	283	386	493	293	395	1.9	3.5	2.3
All employees	466	272	371	477	284	381	2.4	4.4	2.7

Source: New Earnings Survey, Office for National Statistics

persistently low incomes and be more vulnerable to falling into poverty. These disadvantages partly stem from the fact that women are much more likely than men to have caring responsibilities for dependent children and be concentrated in low paid occupations. In turn, women tend to be the ones who limit careers or earning powers to support children.

Average weekly hours of full-time workers were unchanged at 39.6 hours in the year to April 2003 compared with 2002. Average part-time hours decreased slightly to 19.4 hours from 19.6 in 2002.

Managers and senior officials were the occupational group with the highest average gross annual earnings (£42,164) (Table 3.9). At the other end of the scale, personal service occupations earned £14,146 for the 2002/03 tax year. This major group includes occupations acknowledged to be low paid, such as health care assistants, leisure and travel service occupations and hairdressers.

In the 2003 New Earnings Survey (NES), directors and chief executives of major organisations came top of the earnings league of specific occupations (Table 3.10). The next most

Table **3.9**

Pay and hours[1]: by major occupational group[2], April 2003

Great Britain

	Average gross annual pay (£)[3]	Average gross weekly pay (£)	Average total weekly hours
Managers and senior officials	42,164	747.5	39.0
Professional occupations	33,741	650.7	36.3
Associate professional and technical occupations	27,627	527.9	38.5
Administrative and secretarial occupations	17,560	338.4	37.5
Skilled trades occupations	21,060	412.4	42.6
Personal service occupations	14,146	282.9	39.2
Sales and customer service occupations	14,912	288.9	38.8
Process, plant and machine operatives	19,113	373.8	44.8
Elementary occupations	15,825	306.0	42.6
All occupations	25,170	475.8	39.6

1 Employees on adult rates whose pay for the survey period was unaffected by absence.
2 Occupational group (SOC 2000). See Appendix, Part 3: SOC 2000.
3 Annual earnings estimates relate to employees who have been in the same job for at least 12 months, regardless of whether or not their pay was affected by absence.

Source: New Earnings Survey, Office for National Statistics

Table **3.10**

Highest and lowest paid occupations[1], 2003

Great Britain

		Average gross weekly pay (£)
Highest paid		
1	Directors and chief executives of major organisations	2,301.2
2	Medical practitioners	1,186.4
3	Financial managers and chartered secretaries	1,124.2
4	Solicitors and lawyers, judges and coroners	925.8
5	Marketing and sales managers	888.6
6	Information and communication technology managers	872.4
7	Management consultants, actuaries, economists and statisticians	863.1
8	Police officers (inspectors and above)	863.1
9	IT strategy and planning professionals	844.4
10	Financial and accounting technicians	838.1
Lowest paid		
1	Retail cashiers and check-out operators	207.6
2	Launderers, dry cleaners, pressers	217.6
3	Bar staff	217.9
4	Waiters, waitresses	218.2
5	Kitchen and catering assistants	228.4
6	Hotel porters	229.9
7	Hairdressers, barbers	231.8
8	Animal care occupations (not elsewhere classified)	232.3
9	Sewing machinists	239.8
10	Shelf fillers	241.5

1 *Full-time employees on adult rates whose pay for the survey period was unaffected by absence.*

Source: New Earnings Survey, Office for National Statistics

highly paid group was medical practitioners with average gross weekly earnings of £1,186 per week. Though other high earning occupations were represented in the survey, low sample numbers mean that these do not appear in Table 3.10. With average gross weekly earnings of £208, retail desk and check-out operators were the lowest paid of all full-time adult employees.

Worklessness

Lack of participation in the labour market is an important indicator of social exclusion, but it is also an important factor in leading to other aspects of social exclusion, including poverty, homelessness, physical and mental health. For example, poor health can increase the risk of unemployment and economic inactivity and vice versa. The impacts of unemployment are not just immediate, but can also be long term and can influence life chances even during subsequent periods of employment.

Unemployment during the early 1970s was relatively low at around four per cent or one million of the population aged 16 and over (Figure 3.11 - see overleaf). Since then there have been two peaks in unemployment linked to economic recession. In 1984 it peaked at 12 per cent (over 3.2 million) and following an improvement through the late 1980s and early 1990s, it peaked again at 10.9 per cent (3 million) in 1992. There have been gradual improvements over the last decade, levelling off at 5.1 per cent unemployed (1.5 million) in spring 2003.

Unemployment for women and men has followed the same pattern, though male employment was more affected by the recessions in the 1980s and 1990s. In spring 2003, male unemployment was 5.6 per cent, a low level not seen since 1980; female unemployment was 4.5 per cent, close to a record low.

Figure **3.11**

Unemployment rates[1]: by sex[2]

United Kingdom

Percentages

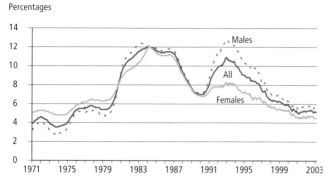

1 Seasonally adjusted. Pre-1992 data are taken from the ONS
   Experimental LFS-Consistent Time Series. See Appendix, Part 3: LFS
   Experimental Time Series.
2 Unemployment rates for working age people: men aged 16 to 64 and
   women aged 16 to 59.

Source: Labour Force Survey, Office for National Statistics

Unemployment is a much greater problem among young adults than among the population aged 25 and over. The unemployment rate for 18 to 24 year old men has fallen by more than a third over the last decade (Figure 3.12). But it is now three times the rate for workers over 50, which fell by two thirds over the same period. The pattern for women is also similar.

Figure **3.12**

Male unemployment rates[1]: by age

United Kingdom

Percentages

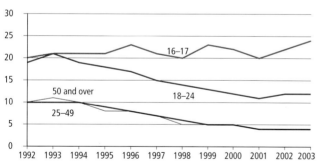

1 Spring quarters, seasonally adjusted.

Source: Labour Force Survey, Office for National Statistics

From the early 1990s the rise in employment for disadvantaged groups has been accompanied by a fall in unemployment (Table 3.13). Nonetheless, with the exception of those aged over 50 with an unemployment rate of three per cent in spring 2003, the disadvantaged groups still have unemployment rates above the overall UK rate of five per cent. For minority ethnic groups the unemployment rate was 11 per cent, for lone parents and those with the lowest qualifications the rate was 10 per cent,

Table **3.13**

Unemployment rates[1]: by disadvantaged groups

United Kingdom   Percentages

	1994	1999	2003
Older people[2]	9	5	3
30 LAs[3]	15	12	9
Minority ethnic groups	21	13	11
Lone parents	18	15	10
Low qualifications[4]	16	12	10
Disabled	..	11	8
All	10	6	5

1 Unemployment rates for working age people: men aged 16 to 64 and
   women aged 16 to 59. Spring quarters. Data are not Census adjusted.
2 Those aged 50 to 64 for men and 50 to 59 for women.
3 People living in the 30 local authority districts with the poorest initial
   labour market position.
4 Those with no formal qualifications.

Source: Department for Work and Pensions, HM Treasury from Labour Force Survey

for the people living in the 30 most disadvantaged local authorities it was 9 per cent and for the disabled it was 8 per cent.

The employed and the unemployed together are described as the economically *active*. The remainder are the economically *inactive*: those who do not want to work, are not seeking work or are not available to work. Patterns over the last thirty years reflect the economic cycle and the changing structure of the workforce (Figure 3.14). In the 1970s the working-age inactivity rate was around 21–22 per cent, a level to which it returned during the 1990s following some fluctuation around the recessions of the 1980s and 1990s. Increases in economic inactivity among certain groups is a serious issue for many economic and social reasons, particularly because of the problems of poverty and welfare dependency experienced among certain groups that have high levels of inactivity, for example those living in workless households.

In spring 2003, the proportion of inactive people of working age was over four times that of the unemployed: 21 per cent compared with five per cent. In 1984 the equivalent ratio was just over two to one. The difference is due to a much lower level of unemployment in 2003 compared with 1984 and inactivity remaining almost constant. The growth in the relative size of the inactive group is particularly remarkable when it is considered that this has occurred among the population of working age. Demographic changes resulting in an increase in the number of older people above state pension age cannot therefore fully explain these changes.

Figure **3.14**

Economic inactivity rates[1]: by sex[2]

United Kingdom

Percentages

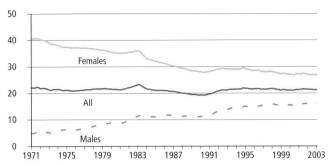

1 Seasonally adjusted. Pre-1992 data are taken from the ONS Experimental LFS-Consistent Time Series. See Appendix, Part 3: LFS Experimental Time Series.
2 Economic inactivity rates for working age people: men aged 16 to 64 and women aged 16 to 59.

Source: Labour Force Survey, Office for National Statistics

Underlying the overall rate are different trends in male and female economic inactivity (Figure 3.14). Female inactivity has continued to decline, from around 41 per cent in 1971 to a rate of 27 per cent in 2003, as more women move into the labour market. At the same time, men have been systematically withdrawing from the labour force such that at spring 2003 around 16 per cent were classified as inactive, more than three times the levels of the early 1970s when it was around five per cent. This is most apparent in the older working-age groups, that is, those aged above 50 (Figure 3.15) and those with lower levels of education and/or skills. The experience of men in this regard is not only linked to the economic cycle but reflects more fundamental changes in the labour market. A major force driving these changes has been the collapse in demand for unskilled workers since the late 1970s.[3] Underlying this collapse has been the rapid expansion of the production and export of low skill goods by developing countries and the bias of technical change in favour of the skilled. This has hit particularly badly those with an additional disadvantage, namely long-term illness or disability. The largest group of economically inactive people among the youngest age group is made up of students in full-time education. As more people stay in education for longer, the student group as a proportion of the working-age population is increasing. Students represent a large number of potential workers, highly likely to participate in the labour market at some time in the future.

In spring 2003 among the economically inactive, the largest difference between the sexes relates to family responsibilities (Table 3.16). Women were more likely to be inactive as a result of looking after a family compared with men of the same age. Economically inactive males as noted above were more likely to

Figure **3.15**

Inactivity rates[1]: by age

United Kingdom

Percentages

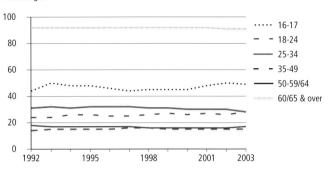

1 Spring quarters. Data not seasonally adjusted.

Source: Labour Force Survey, Office for National Statistics

be long-term sick or disabled. There is an additional group of older men who are economically inactive due to early retirement.[4]

Rates of inactivity are substantially higher than rates of unemployment. This pattern can be seen for the total working-age population as well as for each of the disadvantaged groups. Rising employment has not been accompanied by a

Table **3.16**

Main reason for economic inactivity: by age and sex, spring 2003[1]

United Kingdom Percentages

	16 to 24	25 to 34	35 to 49	50 to 59/64
Males				
Long term sick	4	40	60	42
Looking after family	1	11	16	3
Students	84	24	5	0
Retired	0	0	1	23
Other	11	26	18	32
Total	100	100	100	100
Females				
Long term sick	3	8	25	35
Looking after family	23	75	59	25
Students	65	8	4	1
Retired	0	0	0	13
Other	9	9	12	27
Total	100	100	100	100

1 Data are not Census adjusted.

Source: Labour Market Trends, October 2003 (see reference 4)

substantial fall in inactivity for these groups. The exception to this has been lone parents among whom inactivity has fallen, and people with low or no qualifications among whom inactivity has risen (although as noted, the size of this group is falling quite rapidly) (Table 3.17).

Table **3.17**

Inactivity rates[1]: by disadvantaged groups

United Kingdom			Percentages
	1994	1999	2003
Older people[2]	31	31	28
30 LAs[3]	30	32	31
Minority ethnic groups	35	35	35
Lone parents	49	43	40
Low qualifications[4]	36	43	44
Disabled	..	48	46
All	22	21	21

1 Economic inactivity rates for working age people: men aged 16 to 64 and women aged 16 to 59. Spring quarters. Data are not Census adjusted.
2 Those aged 50 to 64 for men and 50 to 59 for women.
3 People living in the 30 local authority districts with the poorest initial labour market position.
4 Those with no formal qualifications.

Source: Department for Work and Pensions, HM Treasury from Labour Force Survey

Men and women from non-White ethnic groups were more likely than their White counterparts to be economically inactive. The 2001/02 Annual Labour Force Survey showed Bangladeshi and Chinese men had high economic inactivity rates - 31 per cent for each group. However the reasons for inactivity among these two groups were very different. Three quarters of Chinese men were students' compared with just under half of inactive Bangladeshi men; two fifths of inactive Bangladeshi men were long-term sick or disabled. Bangladeshi and Pakistani women had the highest female economic inactivity rates (78 per cent and 72 per cent respectively). The majority of these women were looking after the family or home. White British men and women had the lowest economic inactivity rates (15 per cent and 26 per cent respectively). Within each ethnic group women were more likely than men to be economically inactive.

Workless households

Worklessness becomes a particular problem when concentrated in households where no adult works. So while the UK continues to enjoy high levels of employment, it also has high relative levels of people living in workless households. Nonetheless, most UK households are work rich (58 per cent in

spring 2003), that is, households that include at least one person of working age and where all people of working age are in employment. As previously noted, problems of poverty and social exclusion are prevalent in the vast majority of workless households and there is a link between low income and social exclusion. The predominant factor in reducing poverty among working-age households in recent years has been the growth in employment. Improved access to paid employment for women has increased the number of two-earner households. This, however, has been offset by a substantial rise in the number of no-earner households.[5] In part this is attributable to the high proportion of lone parents without a job and the absolute growth in one-person households.

Though the workless household rate has fallen over recent years, in spring 2003 nearly one in six households containing working-age adults had no one in employment: 4.3 million adults and 1.8 million children were living in these households. Most of these households were dependent on benefit payments. Figure 3.18 shows trends in recent years in the rates of worklessness for the main household types.

Figure **3.18**

Workless households[1]: by household composition

United Kingdom

Percentages

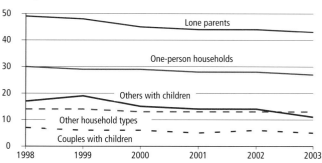

1 Rates for working age people: men aged 16 to 64 and women aged 16 to 59. Spring quarters. Data not Census adjusted.

Source: Labour Force Survey, Office for National Statistics

There is a very low risk of low income in households with two workers. However, 17 per cent of households with one full-time worker have low income and over a third of all low-income households have someone working. The proportion of lone-parent households with dependent children that were workless fell between spring 1998 and spring 2003, from 49 per cent to 43 per cent. Earnings comprise the major component of income for most households and, not surprisingly, those with the highest risk of low income are the unemployed and the economically inactive.[6]

As employment has risen, unemployment rates have fallen. However, the same general decline has not been evident in inactivity rates across regions. Higher rates of inactivity generally exist in areas with above average unemployment rates; however, differences in worklessness between regions primarily reflect variations in inactivity (Figure 3.19). London is the region with the greatest variation between local authorities. The local authority in London with the lowest working-age inactivity rate is Richmond upon Thames (15.4 per cent). Overall in Great Britain, Newham had the highest inactivity rate of all local authorities in 2003 (39.9 per cent). The lowest working-age inactivity rate was 9.6 per cent in Cherwell, in the South East.

Figure **3.19**

Inactivity and unemployment rates[1]: by government office regions, spring 2003

United Kingdom
Percentages

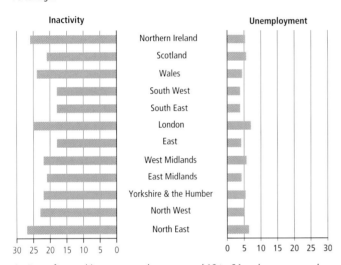

A lack of labour demand is by no means the main explanation for either high unemployment or the numbers claiming benefit. Although the general tendency is for areas with a large number of jobs to have fewer people on both unemployment and inactivity benefits, the relationship is weak. In cities in particular a large number of people claiming benefits can exist with a high number of jobs and vacancies. This is particularly true in inner London where pockets of unemployment exist in areas with significant numbers of available jobs.

European comparisons

Figure 3.20 shows the range of levels of unemployment for working-age men and women in 17 European countries for

2003. The UK unemployment rate of 5 per cent was below the EU-25 average of around 9 per cent. The lowest unemployment levels were found in Luxembourg, the Netherlands, Switzerland, Norway and Austria with rates of around 4 per cent, while the highest rates were in Spain (11 per cent) and Germany (10 per cent). The more southern European countries (such as Spain, Greece and Italy) tend to have both higher inactivity and unemployment rates whereas the more northern countries (such as Denmark, the Netherlands, Norway, Sweden and the UK) tend to have lower unemployment and inactivity. This general pattern almost exactly reflects employment rates.

Figure **3.20**

Unemployment rates[1]: selected European countries, 2003

Percentages

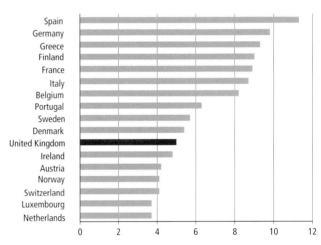

1 Rates for working age people: men aged 15 to 64 and women aged 15 to 59, except UK where rates for working age people are: men aged 16 to 64 and women aged 16 to 59.

Source: EU Labour Force Survey, Eurostat

These patterns may be partly a reflection of differences in the social and political structures across Europe. For example, the highest proportions that are classified as inactive due to personal and family responsibilities, such as childcare, are found in the more southern European countries including Italy, Greece and Spain. The highest rates of inactivity due to illness or disability are found in Denmark, Norway and the UK. High levels of inactive people in the retired group are more common in Denmark, Finland, Austria and Germany. Clearly there are a number of complex factors interacting to determine the levels and reasons for inactivity in Europe, and further analysis would be needed to investigate the impact of these factors on individual sub-groups of the population.

Disadvantaged groups

The remainder of this chapter describes in more detail aspects of the labour market position of some of the groups identified as having high labour market disadvantage: lone parents, those with health conditions or a disability, older workers, minority ethnic groups and, finally, those with multiple disadvantages.

Lone parents

In spring 2003 lone-parent households contained nearly a quarter of all children in the United Kingdom. Until recently many of these families faced extremely high rates of poverty and worklessness. Among lone-parent households with dependent children, the proportion that are workless is 43 per cent (or just under 700,000 households, shown in Figure 3.18), much higher than the overall household rate of 16 per cent. However, this rate is an improvement on a peak of 54 per cent in the early 1990s when the overall rate for all households was 18 per cent.

In the UK, lone mothers are less likely to have a job than mothers in couple families. Since children tend to stay with their mothers when parents separate, the relationship between gender and child poverty can therefore be reinforced on family break-up. This can then be compounded if lone mothers are forced to make further sacrifices in terms of job prospects to meet additional family responsibilities. The costs of appropriate childcare are significant in the UK, creating a further hurdle for mothers on return to the workplace. However, it has been estimated that seven per cent more lone parents are now working at least 16 hours per week in order to claim tax credits.[7] Hours of work among those already working over 16 hours appear to be broadly constant and the employment gains appear not to have come at the expense of an increase in low earners. The remaining non-working lone parents are those who are less skilled and concentrated in rented housing, a group for whom working incentives remain weak.

People with health conditions or disability

The proportion of people of working age reporting a disability has risen in recent years (see Appendix, Part 3: Disability). Over 7 million people of working age are estimated to be disabled (4 million men and 3 million women in spring 2003) and just over half of these are in the labour force (Table 3.21). Approximately half of the disabled population in the UK are economically inactive (43 per cent of men and 51 per cent of women) compared with only 15 per cent for people who are not disabled (10 per cent for men and 22 per cent for women). This demonstrates the employment gap between disabled people

Table 3.21

Economic activity status[1]: by sex and whether disabled[2], spring 2003[3]

United Kingdom

Percentages

	Males		Females		All	
	Disabled	Not disabled	Disabled	Not disabled	Disabled	Not disabled
Economically active						
In employment	51.4	85.8	45.9	75.3	48.8	80.8
Unemployed	5.5	4.4	3.1	3.0	4.4	3.8
All economically active	56.9	90.3	49.0	78.3	53.2	84.6
Unemployment rate[4]	9.6	4.9	6.4	3.9	8.2	4.5
Economically inactive						
Wants a job	14.9	2.4	14.6	5.2	14.7	3.7
Does not want a job	28.2	7.4	36.4	16.5	32.1	11.7
All economically inactive	43.1	9.7	51.0	21.7	46.8	15.4

1 Males aged 16 to 64, females aged 16 to 59.
2 Current long-term health problem or disability.
3 Data are not seasonally adjusted and have not been adjusted to take account of the Census 2001 results. See Appendix, Part 3: Labour Force Survey data.
4 The percentage of economically active people who are unemployed.

Source: Labour Force Survey, Office for National Statistics

and the rest of the population. In the case of people with disabilities, factors affecting an individual's ability or willingness to supply their labour are likely to include: the severity of the disability; access to and within a potential workplace; beliefs about the likelihood of facing discrimination; beliefs about the availability of suitable jobs; and also the trade-off between employment income and benefit receipt. People with particular disabilities, of course, cannot fulfil certain jobs.

It is important to note that although the numbers reporting disabilities have increased quite markedly in recent decades, this is likely to be, at least in part, a result of higher reporting, for example, as a result of increased public awareness about different types of disability.

Older workers

Men aged 50 to 64 and women aged 50 to 59 are a group that is attracting considerable research interest and a number of studies have been recently published that focus on aspects of work and retirement. Findings have highlighted the following:[8]

- Training and worker development remains skewed towards younger workers.

- Workers in professional and managerial jobs tend to enjoy greater choice and control over how they leave the workforce.

- Financial factors tend not to be the primary force driving decisions about leaving work; however, these are likely to be a key constraint determining when it is possible to do so.

- Ceasing work early increases the long-term risk of poverty for some occupational groups, but it is less important than one's overall work history. Those with modest means, but not the poorest workers, have a particular risk of a substantial drop in income between early job exit and state pension age.

- People who leave permanent full-time jobs before state pension age are as likely to move initially into part-time, temporary or self-employed work as to leave the workforce directly. However, opportunities to get good 'bridge' jobs of this type tend to be much greater for certain groups than others.

- People with negative experiences on leaving work, and those in financial difficulties, are less likely to engage in fulfilling activities in retirement, such as involvement in the community.

Other research has explored the factors that encourage labour market participation and influence labour market withdrawal among this age group.[9] For many it is clear that the current state pension age is seen as the 'natural' time to retire, though there are sizeable segments that would choose to work later (20 per cent of the research sample) or to retire early (20 per cent of the sample).

Minority ethnic groups

Minority ethnic groups make up about eight per cent of the population and they tend to be clustered in Britain's major cities and conurbations. Minority ethnic groups have a younger age profile than the population as a whole and, as a result, they are expected to account for over half the growth in Britain's working-age population between 1999 and 2009.[10] Certain minority ethnic groups appear to be significantly disadvantaged in the UK labour market. They experience considerable additional unemployment risks and earnings gaps and these often lead to major material consequences. Limited economic opportunities are closely bound up with social exclusion.

During the period 2002/03 the overall employment rate for people from minority ethnic backgrounds was 58 per cent compared with around 74 per cent for the UK population (Table 3.22 – see overleaf). Within the minority ethnic population as a whole, there are disparities between the employment rates of different ethnic groups and between genders within the ethnic groups and it is important to consider the different groups separately. People of Indian origin have employment rates that are not far behind those of White people, whereas people of Bangladeshi, Pakistani and Mixed origin tend to have higher rates of unemployment.

Employment rates for British-born minority ethnic groups and immigrants are generally lower than those of British-born Whites with the same age and level of educational qualification. Research has shown that relative employment prospects have improved for some groups, mostly among minority ethnic groups born in Britain.[11] There are notable exceptions to this, however, as employment rates for British-born African-Caribbean and Bangladeshi men appear to have declined, despite general improvements in the economy.

The factors behind these differences are multiple and complex and include education and skills, the ability to gain access to employment opportunities, and discrimination in the workplace. For women from certain groups, cultural or religious factors may also influence their labour market position. Much more information is needed on this topic;

Table **3.22**

Economic activity status rates by ethnic group[1], 2002/03[2]

United Kingdom   Percentages

	Employment rate	Unemployment rate
Total population[2]	74	5
White	76	5
British	76	5
Irish	72	4
Other White	71	6
Mixed	60	15
Asian or Asian British	56	10
Indian	68	7
Pakistani	45	15
Bangladeshi	39	17
Other Asian	57	10
Black or Black British	60	13
Black Caribbean	66	12
Black African	54	13
Other Black[3]	61	13
Chinese[3]	57	7
Other ethnic group	53	12
All minority ethnic groups	58	11

1 See Appendix, Part 3: Ethnic group classifications. Rates for working age people: men aged 16 to 64 and women aged 16 to 59.
2 The total population includes people who did not state their ethnic group.
3 The sample size for the unemployed in these ethnic categories is not large enough to generate a fully reliable estimate. Therefore the figures in these groups are only indicative.

Source: Annual Local Area Labour Force Survey, Office for National Statistics

however, there is an acknowledged lack of data that inhibits more detailed analysis of the issues being faced by minority ethnic groups, particularly at a regional or local level and within individual groups.

Multiple disadvantage

In considering disadvantage, it is clear that individuals can belong to more than one disadvantaged group. Workless lone-parents, or people with disabilities, for example, tend to have low or no qualifications. Recent research suggests that the more disadvantages facing an individual, the greater the likelihood that he or she will not be employed.[12] Some working-age families in Britain experience combinations of disadvantage, which means that they are almost certain to have no work.

Those most at risk of non-employment are:

1. lone parents

2. disabled people

3. people with low or no qualifications and skills

4. people aged over 50

5. people living in the most deprived areas

6. members of minority ethnic groups.

Two thirds of adults in Britain have at least one of these six disadvantages and about a tenth have two of them. Very few (1 in 5,000) have all six. The more of these disadvantages people have, the greater the risk of them not being employed. Their poor prospects can be explained largely in terms of the cumulative effects of each of their specific disadvantages. The number of barriers faced by individuals does not seem to be an issue in its own right. The 'additive' pattern of disadvantage suggests that gains can be made by tackling the barriers to employment in a systematic way.

Conclusion

The United Kingdom is experiencing very high rates of employment, very low rates of unemployment and record numbers in work. In recent years there have been relative improvements for a number of key sections of the population. Women's participation in the labour market has increased and there have been relative improvements in terms of the number and types of jobs available and improved earnings potential. However children affect the economic activity of women more than men. Women with young children are around half as likely as men with young children to be in employment.

A substantial proportion of adults in the UK report at least one of the six labour market disadvantages – being a lone parent, aged over 50, from a minority ethnic group, with low or no formal qualifications, disabled, or living in one of the 30 most disadvantaged local authorities. Despite increases in employment among people in these groups, they remain around twice as likely to be unemployed compared with the total working age population. The likelihood of labour force participation declines with multiple disadvantages.

Government policy

Since the election of the new Labour government in 1997, a policy of active labour market policies has been pursued with an overarching aim of ensuring that all who are able to move into work should be able to do so. It has three broad themes:

- providing active, work-focused support

- ensuring work pays

- reducing barriers to work

Under the Welfare to Work programme, various initiatives have been taken forward aimed at helping the most disadvantaged and vulnerable groups within the labour market. Jobcentre Plus was launched in 2002.

New Deals are an integral part of government strategy. These are designed to tackle long-term unemployment by helping people find jobs and improving long term employability. There are a large number of new deals including those for young people (NDYP), for those aged 25 and over (ND25+), for those aged 50 and over (ND50+) and disabled people (NDDP).

The National Minimum Wage (effective from April 1999) and the Working Tax Credit and Child Tax Credit are the key policies aimed at making work pay.

In January 2003 the government set up the Disability Employment Advisory Committee (www.deac.org.uk) to consider and advise on how disabled people can be supported to find and keep work.

In March 2003 *Ethnic minorities and the Labour Market* was published. This outlined a strategy for targeted action to meet the needs of different ethnic groups. The Government has pledged to ensure that no one faces disproportionate barriers to achievement in the labour market because of their ethnicity and DWP and the Department for Trade and Industry (DTI) share a PSA target to increase the employment rates of people from minority ethnic backgrounds.

The Employment Act of 2002 gives more rights to temporary employees and generally aims to promote the economic benefits of work-life balance.

Government reforms for lone parents have concentrated on an improved range of Job Centre services, raising welfare payments (in and out of work) and improving financial incentives to work, including accessible and affordable childcare.

Anti-discrimination is another important theme for this government and various initiatives are being introduced to help groups as diverse as older people, the disabled and those from minority ethnic populations.

Glossary of terms

Measures are based on International Labour Organisation (ILO) guidelines used in the Labour Force Survey.

Economically active:	those who are in work or training or actively seeking and available for work. This includes employed and unemployed people.
In employment :	a measure obtained from household surveys and censuses, of employees, self-employed people, participants in Government employment and training programmes, and people doing unpaid family work.
Unemployed:	the measure counts as unemployed those who are out of work, want a job and have been actively looking for one in the past four weeks. They must also be available to start a job in the next fortnight or be waiting to start a job already obtained.
Unemployment rate:	the percentage of the economically active who are unemployed.
Economically inactive:	those who are neither in employment nor unemployment. This includes the retired, those looking after a home and those who are unable to work due to long-term sickness or disability.
Working-age household:	a household that includes at least one person of working age, that is, a man between the ages of 16 and 64 and a women between 16 and 59.
Workless household:	a household that includes at least one person of working age where no-one aged 16 or over is in employment

References

1. HM Treasury & Department for Work & Pensions (2003). *Full employment in every region.* The Stationery Office

2. Cully M, Woodland S, O'Reilly A and Dix G (1999). *Britain at Work.* Routledge

3. Faggio G and Nickel S (2003). *The rise in inactivity among adult men* (Chapter 3 pp 40-52, Dickens, Gregg and Wadsworth (Eds) 2003)

4. Barham C (October 2003). Life stages of economic inactivity. *Labour Market Trends.* The Stationery Office

5. Gregg P and Wadsworth J (1998). *Unemployment and non-employment; Unpacking economic inactivity.* Employment Policy Institute

6. Department for Work & Pensions (2003). *Opportunity for all.* Fifth annual report. The Stationery Office

7. Gregg P and Harkness S (2003). *Welfare reform and the employment of lone parents* (Chapter 7 pp 98-115, Dickens, Gregg and Wadsworth (Eds) 2003)

8. Foundations (December 2003). *Crossroads after 50.* Joseph Rowntree Foundation

9. Humphrey A, Costigan P, Pickering K, Stratford N and Barnes M (2003). *Factors affecting the labour market participation of older workers.* DWP Research report 200, The Stationery Office

10. Cabinet Office, Strategy Unit (2003). *Ethnic minorities and the labour market*

11. Wadsworth J (2003). *The labour market performance of ethnic minorities in the recovery* (Chapter 8 pp 116 – 133, Dickens, Gregg and Wadsworth (Eds) 2003)

12. Bertoud R (2002). *Multiple disadvantage in the labour market.* Joseph Rowntree Foundation. York Publishing Services

Further reading

Bulman J (October 2003). Patterns of pay: results of the 2003 New Earnings Survey, *Labour Market Trends*

Dickens R, Gregg P and Wadsworth J (Eds) (2003). *The labour market under new Labour, The State of Working Britain.* Palgrave Macmillan

Lindsay C and Doyle P (September 2003). Experimental consistent time series of historical Labour Force Survey data. *Labour Market Trends.* The Stationery Office

Palmer G, North J, Carr J and Kenway P (2003). *Monitoring poverty and social exclusion.* New Policy Institute. Joseph Rowntree Foundation

Income

Jenny Church

Chapter 4

Introduction

This chapter explores inequalities in the distribution of income and of wealth. Inequality in the distribution of income is important to the understanding of inequality more generally in two senses. Firstly, income provides the ability to gain access to goods and services which affect people's standard of living in many different ways. Secondly, differences in income are often the result of other inequalities discussed elsewhere in this publication, because people's incomes depend on factors such as their labour market participation, health status, educational attainment, and so on; factors which are themselves interrelated.

Although the terms 'wealth' and 'income' are often used interchangeably, in economic terms they refer to rather different concepts. Whereas income represents a flow of resources over a period of time, wealth is the term used for the ownership of assets, valued at a point in time. However, inequality in the distribution of wealth is important to the understanding of income inequality because wealth may provide a flow of current income (for example, interest on savings accounts or dividends from shares), or it may provide entitlement to a future income flow (for example, pension rights).

Income

Income distribution

The picture of the income distribution in Great Britain in 2002/03, summarised in Figure 4.1, shows considerable inequality. Each bar represents the number of people living in households with equivalised weekly disposable income (see Appendix, Part 4: Equivalisation scales) in a particular £5 band. There is clearly a greater concentration of people at the lower levels of weekly income and the distribution has a long tail at the upper end. The upper tail is in fact longer than shown: there are estimated to be an additional 1.6 million individuals living in households with more than £1,000 per week which are not shown on the graph. The highest bar represents nearly 0.9 million people with incomes between £220 and £225 per week. If housing costs are deducted, the concentration of incomes towards the lower end of the distribution is even greater, because housing costs for low-income households form on average a higher proportion of their income.

An alternative way of examining the degree of inequality is to calculate the shares of total disposable income received by equal sized groups of the population when ranked by their income. If income were evenly distributed each group would

Figure **4.1**

Distribution of weekly household income[1], 2002/03

Great Britain

Number of individuals (millions)

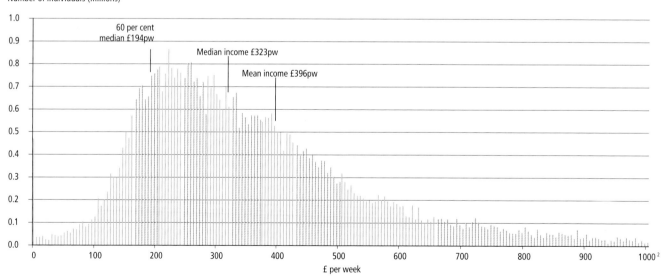

1 Equivalised household disposable income before housing costs (in £5 bands). See Appendix, Part 4: Equivalisation scales.
2 There were also 1.6 million individuals with income above £1,000 per week.

Source: Households Below Average Income, Department for Work and Pensions

Figure **4.2**

Shares of total disposable income[1], 2002/03

Great Britain

Percentages

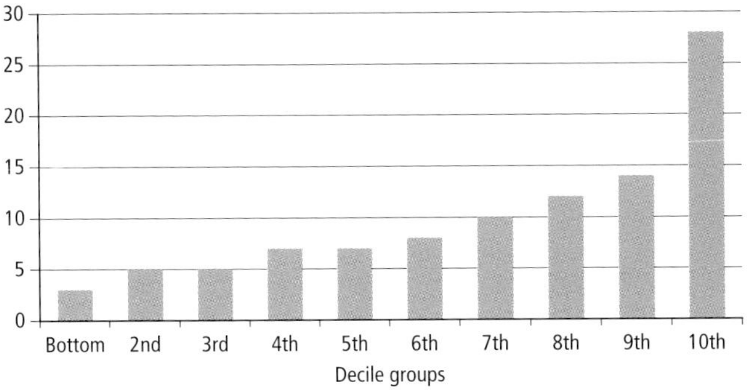

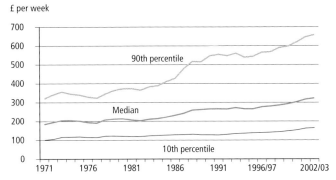

1 Equivalised household disposable income before housing costs has been used to rank individuals. See Appendix, Part 4: Equivalisation scales.

Source: Households Below Average Income, Department for Work and Pensions

Figure **4.3**

Distribution of real[1] disposable household income[2,3]

United Kingdom/Great Britain

£ per week

1 Data adjusted to 2002/03 prices using the Retail Prices Index less local taxes.
2 Equivalised household disposable income before housing costs. See Appendix, Part 4: Equivalisation scales.
3 Source data changed in 1994/95 from FES to HBAI series, definition of income changed slightly and geographic coverage changed from United Kingdom to Great Britain. Data from 1993/94 onwards are for financial years.

Source: Institute for Fiscal Studies from Family Expenditure Survey; Households Below Average Income, Department for Work and Pensions

receive the same share. Figure 4.2 shows that this is far from the case: the top decile group (see Appendix, Part 4: Quartiles, quintiles and deciles) accounted for 28 per cent of total income in 2002/03; if there was complete equality each group would account for 10 per cent. In fact the first seven decile groups received nearly half of total income, with the other half going to the top three decile groups.

The shape of the income distribution and the extent of inequality have changed considerably over the last three decades. In Figure 4.3, the closer the 90th and 10th percentiles and the median lines, the greater the equality within the distribution. During the early 1970s, the distribution seems to have been broadly stable. Between about 1973 and 1979 there was a gradual decrease in inequality, but this was reversed during the early 1980s and the extent of inequality in the distribution continued to grow throughout the 1980s. Between 1981 and 1989, average (median) income (adjusted for inflation) rose by 27 per cent. In contrast, income at the 90th percentile rose by 38 per cent and that at the 10th percentile by only seven per cent. During the first half of the 1990s the income distribution appeared to be stable again, albeit at a much higher level of income dispersion than in the 1960s. It should be recalled that the first half of the 1990s was a period of economic downturn when there was little real growth in incomes anywhere in the distribution. Between 1994/95 and 2002/03, income at the 90th and 10th percentiles and at the median all grew by over a fifth in real terms, though on some measures such as the Gini coefficient there appears to have been a further small increase in inequality.

The Institute for Fiscal Studies (IFS) has investigated some of the possible explanations for the changes in inequality seen

over the last two decades, and in particular why the trends are different over the economic cycles of the 1980s and 1990s.[1] They found that wage growth played a part: inequality tends to rise during periods of rapid wage growth because the poorest households are the most likely to contain non-working individuals. The economic recovery in the 1980s was characterised by large increases in wages in each of the years from 1984 to 1988 matching the period when inequality increased rapidly. In contrast wage growth was very slow to return in the recovery of the early to mid-1990s – a time of stable or falling inequality. Growth in self-employment income and in unemployment were also found to be associated with periods of increased inequality. It would appear that demographic factors such as the growth in one-person households make a relatively unimportant contribution compared with labour market changes. However, the IFS have found that changes in the tax and benefit system have an impact in accordance with what economic theory would suggest: the income tax cuts of the 1970s and late 1980s worked to increase income inequality, while direct tax rises in the early 1980s and 1990s together with the increases in means-tested benefits in the late 1990s produced the opposite effect.

However, IFS research also indicates that the slight increase in inequality between 1996/97 and 2002/03 is very different in nature from that observed over the 1980s. During the 1980s the higher the income, the greater was income growth and it was this that drove the increase in inequality. However, between 1996/97 and 2002/03, income growth has been much more evenly spread across the whole of the income distribution, with exceptions only at the very top and bottom of the distribution. Changes at the very bottom of the distribution are difficult to disentangle from measurement error. However, there is evidence not only from these data based on the Family Resources Survey (FRS), but also from data from tax returns, that there has indeed been much more rapid growth in the top one per cent of incomes than for the rest of the distribution. The reasons for this growth are not yet well understood, but possible explanations include changes in the nature of executive remuneration and the dynamic effects of the cut in top rates of tax over the 1980s on capital accumulation.[2]

According to the British Social Attitudes Survey, a high proportion of people in Great Britain consider that the gap between those with high incomes and those with low incomes is too large: 72 per cent in 1983, and more than 80 per cent from 1989 onwards, peaking at 87 per cent in 1995. In 2002, the latest available year, the proportion stood at 82 per cent. In 2002, concern about the income gap was expressed by around three quarters or more of each social class and income group, though people in less advantaged positions (for example, with low incomes or working class occupations) are more likely to consider that income gaps are too large.

There is a higher degree of inequality within the United Kingdom's income distribution than for most other EU Member States. Using data from the European Community Household Panel Survey (ECHP), the ratio of the shares of total income received by the top and bottom quintile groups for the United Kingdom was 4.9 in 2001 compared with the EU average of 4.4. Italy was at about the same level as the United Kingdom with a ratio of 4.8, and only Spain, Greece and Portugal recorded higher ratios. Most Member States had ratios between 3 and 4.

Income is important to people's overall well being in terms of the access that it provides to goods and services. Thus people's satisfaction with their income will depend on their material needs and expectations and the extent to which the income available to them enables these to be met. It is therefore possible that individuals with the same level of income but different levels of needs (real or perceived), or faced with different prices for the same level and quality of goods or services (for example, housing), may consider themselves 'well-off' or not so 'well-off'. Table 4.4 explores trends in people's perception of economic hardship or lack of it. The proportion of respondents considering that they were living comfortably rose from 24 per cent in 1984 to 39 per cent in 2002, while the proportion who said they were finding it difficult or very

Table **4.4**

People's perceptions of the adequacy of their income[1]

Great Britain   Percentages

	1986	1989	1994	1998	2002
Living comfortably	24	27	29	37	39
Coping	49	49	49	46	44
Finding it difficult to manage	18	17	16	12	13
Finding it very difficult to manage	8	6	6	4	3

1 Respondents were asked, 'Which of these phrases would you say comes closest to your feelings about your household's income these days? Living comfortably, coping, finding it difficult to manage, or finding it very difficult to manage on present income'.

Source: British Social Attitudes Survey, National Centre for Social Research

difficult to cope had fallen from 26 per cent to 16 per cent. This is of course not necessarily inconsistent with a widening of the distribution – as Figure 4.3 showed, although the 90th, 50th (median) and 10th percentiles have moved apart, they have all increased in real terms.

There are a variety of factors that influence an individual's position in the income distribution. The factors most strongly associated with being in the top quintile group in 2002/03 were being in a couple without children or being in full-time work (Table 4.5). Single person and couple families all in full-time work had twice the expected likelihood of being in this group. Conversely, being unemployed increased the risk of being in the bottom quintile group more than threefold and being economically inactive but under pension age increased the risk two and a half times compared with the average. Most minority ethnic groups had greater than average likelihood of being in the bottom quintile group, with the Pakistani/Bangladeshi group being particularly at risk. Other groups with greater than average risks of being in the bottom quintile group were single parents and families containing both disabled adults and one or more disabled children.

Low incomes

Although being in the bottom quintile or decile group is one way in which to define low income, these definitions are not generally used because of their relative nature. It would mean that 20 or 10 per cent of the population will always be defined as poor. Other approaches generally involve fixing a threshold in monetary terms, below which a household is considered to be 'poor'. This threshold may be calculated in variety of ways. In countries at a very low level of development it may be considered useful to cost the bare essentials to maintain human life and use this as the yardstick against which to measure income. Although this 'basic needs' measure is of limited usefulness for a country such as the United Kingdom, a similar approach is described in Chapter 5: Living Standards, where the inability to afford a set of goods and services considered as 'necessities' by the majority of the population is used to define those in poverty.

However, the approach generally used is to fix an income threshold in terms of a fraction of population median income.

Table 4.5

Risk of falling into the top and bottom quintile groups of household disposable income[1]: by risk factors[2], 2002/03

Great Britain   Percentages

	Bottom quintile	Top quintile
Economic status of adults in the family		
One or more full-time self-employed	19	31
Single/couple all in full-time work	4	37
Couple, one full-time, one part-time working	4	22
Workless, head or spouse aged 60 or over	29	7
Workless, head or spouse unemployed	70	3
Workless, other inactive	51	3
Family type		
Single pensioner, male	21	9
Single pensioner, female	26	7
Couple without children	10	38
Single with children	39	4
Ethnic group of head of household		
Black Caribbean	28	9
Black non-Caribbean	35	11
Pakistani/Bangladeshi	66	3
Disability		
One or more disabled children in family	27	8
of which:		
no disabled adults in family	23	9
one or more disabled adults in family	33	7
All individuals	20	20

1 *Equivalised household disposable income before housing costs has been used to rank individuals. See Appendix, Part 4: Equivalisation scales.*
2 *Factors have been included in this table if they give rise to proportions of individuals falling outside the range 10 percentage points above or below the expected threshold in either the top or bottom quintile group if there was an even distribution.*

Source: Households Below Average Income, Department for Work and Pensions

This threshold may then be fixed in real terms for a number of years, or it may be calculated in respect of the distribution for each successive year. The Government's 'Opportunity for All' (OfA) indicators use both approaches. The proportions of people living in households with incomes below various fractions of contemporary median income are monitored, referred to as those with relative low income, as well as the proportions with incomes below various fractions of median income in 1996/97, known as those with absolute low income. A third OfA indicator measures the number of people with persistent low income, defined as being in a low income household in three out of the last four years. (Discussion of the persistence of low income may be found in the section on Income Mobility below.) In addition, the Government has announced that to monitor progress against its child poverty target, it will add to these measures one that combines material deprivation and relative low income.[3] Deprivation measures resonate well with the public perception of poverty, and it has also been established that there is a strong relationship between material deprivation and persistent low income. As time spent on low income increases, the severity of deprivation increases.

Figure 4.6 uses 60 per cent of contemporary equivalised median household disposable income before the deduction of housing costs as the low-income threshold. In 2002/03, this represented an income of £194 per week, just below the lowest quintile. As well as being one of the OfA indicators, this definition has also been adopted by the Laeken European Council in December 2001 as one of a set of 18 statistical indicators for social inclusion. Using this threshold, the

Figure 4.6

People living in households with income[1,2] below 60 per cent of the median

United Kingdom/Great Britain
Percentages

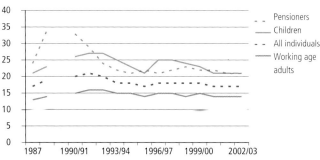

1 *Equivalised household disposable income before housing costs.*
2 *Source data changed in 1994/95 from FES to HBAI series, definition of income changed slightly and geographic coverage changed from United Kingdom to Great Britain. Data for 1988/89 onwards are for financial years.*

Source: Institute for Fiscal Studies from Family Expenditure Survey; Households Below Average Income, Department for Work and Pensions

proportion of the population living in low-income households rose from 12 per cent in 1979 to reach a peak of 21 per cent in 1991/92, since when it has fallen back to 17 per cent in each of the three years 2000/01 to 2002/03.

In a report produced for the Office of the First Minister and Deputy First Minister in Northern Ireland data from Northern Ireland (2002) and Great Britain (2001/02) were compared to assess poverty levels.[4] It found that the proportion of persons living in low-income households (with less than 60 per cent of median income) was around five percentage points higher in Northern Ireland.

In 2001, according to the ECHP, 15 per cent of the population of the EU lived in low-income households measured against the median income of the country in which they live. Sweden had the lowest proportion of households with low income at just nine per cent, compared with Ireland with 21 per cent. The proportion for the United Kingdom using this data source was 17 per cent.

Different groups within the population experience different risks of low income. Figure 4.6 shows that working age adults were generally at lower risk than the population as a whole throughout the period 1979 to 2002/03, though as Table 4.5 has shown there are particular groups within this sub-population who are at much greater risk, in particular those living in workless households. However, the greatest change in risk of low income over this period has been for pensioners. In 2002/03, pensioners had a lower risk of having low income even than in 1979 and an appreciably lower risk than in 1988/89 or in 1990/91, though they are still over-represented in the lower half of the income distribution. Pensioners tend to be higher up the income distribution if income is measured after the deduction of housing costs, because of the high proportion who own their homes outright and for whom therefore housing costs are low relative to their income. Thus when income is measured after the deduction of housing costs pensioners were slightly less likely to face low income than the rest of the population. Because pensioners' state benefit income, primarily the state retirement pension, varies within a fairly narrow range, it is their receipt of occupational pension and investment income which tends to determine their position in the income distribution. In 2002/03, over half of pensioners living in low-income households had no occupational or personal pension income, compared with a third of all pensioners.

In 2002/03, there were 2.6 million children in Great Britain living in low-income households (income measured before the deduction of housing costs). This represented around a fifth of all children, indicating that they were at greater risk of low

income compared with the population as a whole. This proportion peaked in the early 1990s at over a quarter, but in 1979 it was less than an eighth. A number of the high risk factors for children to be living in low-income households are similar to those for the population as a whole: living in workless families or households, living in lone-parent families, and living in families headed by someone from a minority ethnic group, in particular someone of Pakistani/Bangladeshi origin. In addition, there is a clear relationship between the number of children in the family and their position in the income distribution: as the number of children in the family increases, so does the risk of low income. Around 45 per cent of children in families with four or more children were in the low-income group in 2002/03, compared with 15 per cent of those who were the only dependent child.

Sources of income

Table 4.7 explores further the life cycle nature of income by analysing the sources of income on which people rely at different stages in their lives. This table is based on household income and categorises households by the age of the head of household only. There will of course be other household members of different ages whose income contributes to that of the household - for example, young adults living with their middle-aged parents. The table therefore does not give a complete picture of the life cycle trajectory of income but nevertheless provides some useful pointers.

On average, income from work (whether as an employee or self-employed person) forms the largest component for households headed by a person of working age (between the school-leaving age of 16 and state retirement pension age). For households headed by someone under the age of 25, many of whom will still be in full-time education, student loans and other forms of student support together with social benefits are also important income sources. Disability benefits grow in importance with age, as do other Social Security benefits which are least important during the middle years of life. State retirement pensions, other Benefit income and other pensions form the bulk of income for those in households headed by someone over 65. However, private pensions tend to play a less important role for older pensioners. This is partly because there are more women than men in the oldest age groups and they are less likely to have private pension entitlements, and partly because those in the oldest age groups were working at a time when private pensions were less common.

Although having earnings from full-time employed or self-employed work is a major factor reducing the risk of having low household income, there are substantial variations in the levels of people's earnings that determine their position within

Table **4.7**

Components of gross household income by age of head of household, 2002/03

United Kingdom

Percentage of gross weekly income

Age group	Source of income								
	Wages and salaries	Self employ-ment income	Invest-ments	Tax credits	State Retire-ment Pension plus any IS	Other pensions	Social Security disability benefits	Other Social Security benefits	Other sources
16 to 24	63	3	-	2	-	-	1	12	19
25 to 34	82	6	1	2	-	-	1	7	2
35 to 44	77	11	1	1	-	-	1	6	2
45 to 54	76	12	2	-	-	2	2	4	2
55 to 59	66	11	3	-	1	10	3	4	2
60 to 64	44	10	4	-	8	21	5	6	2
65 to 74	12	4	6	-	36	32	4	5	2
75 to 84	6	1	6	-	43	28	6	8	2
85 or over	1	1	6	0	47	23	9	12	2
All households	65	9	2	1	6	7	2	6	3

Source: Family Resources Survey, Department for Work and Pensions

the income distribution. Wage rates can vary considerably between occupational groups and levels of educational attainment (see Chapters 2: Education, training and skills, and 3: Work).

Although income in money terms is the primary means of analysing income inequality, there are a number of non-monetary benefits that people receive from government expenditure on services such as education and health. These services, known as benefits in kind, are funded from government revenue and then provided free at the point of use. If they were not provided in this way then individuals might have to purchase them from their income, as indeed is the case in some countries. Thus in their analysis of the effects of taxes and benefits on household income, the Office for National Statistics (ONS) calculates the imputed income that households receive from a range of benefits in kind.[5] Because households in the bottom quintile group of income tend to benefit more from these services than those in the top group, the addition of this imputed income tends to reduce the degree of inequality in the distribution. In 2002/03, the ratio of average income in the top quintile group to that in the bottom quintile group was 4:1 after the addition of this imputed income compared with 7:1 before its addition.

Income mobility

People's position within the income distribution is not necessarily fixed over time. For example they may move up the distribution during their working years as their careers develop and their earnings rise, but they may then move downwards in retirement. Table 4.8 (see overleaf) shows that 41 per cent of those in the bottom quintile group and 45 per cent of those in the top quintile group in 1991 were also in those groups in 2001. However, only 17 per cent had remained in the top quintile group in each of the eleven years and even fewer (eight per cent) had remained in the bottom group. To move the whole length of the distribution from bottom to top or vice versa is relatively rare. Only seven per cent of individuals in the bottom quintile group in 1991 were in the top group in 2001, and about nine per cent of individuals had moved from the top to the bottom over the period. Thus although the table indicates that there is a considerable degree of mobility within the income distribution, many of these movements are short-term and of short distance.

The implications of this finding on the persistence of low income over time are that relatively few people are likely to spend extended periods in low-income households, but that many may spend short periods on low income. This is confirmed by research by the Department for Work and Pensions using the British Household Panel Survey (BHPS). This

Table **4.8**

Position of individuals in the income distribution in 2001, in relation to their position in 1991

Great Britain   Percentages

Position in 2001	Position in 1991				
	Bottom quintile	Second quintile	Third quintile	Fourth quintile	Top quintile
Bottom quintile	41	24	15	12	9
Second quintile	26	30	22	13	8
Third quintile	16	22	25	22	16
Fourth quintile	10	16	22	29	23
Top quintile	7	8	16	24	45
Total	100	100	100	100	100

Source: Department for Work and Pensions from the British Household Panel Survey, Institute for Social and Economic Research

shows that over the eleven year period 1991 to 2001, only one per cent of individuals spent the whole of that period in households with income below 60 per cent of the median (the same low income threshold as used in Figure 4.6 and therefore measured before the deduction of housing costs). However, 50 per cent of individuals spent at least one year of this period in a low-income household.

Further research using the BHPS has shown that one of the major factors contributing to changes in an individual's position in the income distribution is change in the composition of the family in which they live. For women over the period 1991 to 1999, setting up home with a male partner was more than twice as likely to result in an increase in equivalised household income of one or more quintile groups as it was to result in a fall of one or more quintile groups. Conversely, when they separated from a male partner about half experienced a fall of one or more quintiles, whereas only about one fifth experienced a rise. For men, joining with a female partner is more likely to result in a fall in equivalised household income than it is to result in a rise, whereas separating from them is more likely to result in a rise. In general, changes in family composition have less effect on men's position in the income distribution than on the position of women. These results reflect the higher individual incomes of men compared to women.

There is much debate about the extent of intergenerational transmission of inequality and of deprivation in particular, in other words, the extent to which people's position in the income distribution changes compared with that of their parents. This can be analysed using long-term cohort studies,

such as the National Child Development Survey, a cohort of all individuals born in a week of March 1958. Research using the fairly large samples of parents and children from this data source indicates that the extent of income mobility is limited in terms of both earnings and education among this cohort,[6] confirming that children of parents with high income/qualifications are more likely than other children to have high income/qualifications themselves. The research also found that upward mobility from the bottom of the earnings distribution is more likely than downward mobility from the top.

Wealth, savings and debt

Wealth can be held in the form of financial assets such as savings accounts or shares that provide a flow of current income, or pension rights that provide an entitlement to a future income flow. These types of asset form financial wealth. Ownership of non-financial wealth may also provide financial security even if it does not provide a current income flow: for example, ownership of a house or a work of art that could be sold to provide income if necessary. In this section the term 'wealth' includes both financial and non-financial assets. There is a further distinction sometimes made between marketable and non-marketable wealth. Marketable wealth comprises assets that can be sold and their value realised, whereas non-marketable wealth comprises mainly pension rights which often cannot be 'cashed in'.

Wealth may be accumulated either by the acquisition of new assets through saving or by inheritance, or by the increase in value of existing assets. However, wealth may also be 'drawn down' in times of economic hardship through withdrawals from savings or by the accumulation of debt. Thus wealth, savings and debt are very much interlinked.

Distribution of wealth

Over the 20th century as a whole, the distribution of wealth became more equal. In 1911, it is estimated that the wealthiest one per cent of the population held around 70 per cent of the United Kingdom's wealth. By 1936–38, this proportion had fallen to 56 per cent, and it fell again after World War II to reach 42 per cent in 1960.[7] Table 4.9, using different methodology from the historic data, shows that during the 1970s and 1980s, the share of the wealthiest one per cent of the population fell from around 22 per cent to reach 18 per cent in 1986. Since then the distribution appears to have widened again, with 23 per cent recorded in 2001. Latest data indicate that it remained at this level in 2002.

However, even during the 1970s and 1980s when the distribution was at its most equal, these estimates indicate that

Table 4.9

Distribution of wealth

United Kingdom   Percentages

	1976	1986	1991	1996	2001
Most wealthy 1%	21	18	17	20	23
Most wealthy 25%	71	73	71	74	75
Most wealthy 50%	92	90	92	93	95

Source: Inland Revenue

wealth is very much less evenly distributed than income, half the population owning only five per cent of total wealth in 2001. To some extent this is because of life cycle effects: it usually takes time for people to build up assets during their working lives through savings and then draw them down during the years of retirement with the residue passing to others after their death. If the value of housing is omitted from the wealth estimates, the resulting distribution is even more concentrated at the top of the distribution, indicating that this form of wealth is rather more evenly distributed than the remainder.

A word of warning should be sounded about the reliability of these wealth estimates. They are based on inheritance and capital transfer taxes rather than direct measurement through sample survey. As such they cover only marketable wealth and so some important elements such as pension rights are excluded. Although some surveys carry questions on some elements of wealth, and these are drawn on below, there is currently no comprehensive source of data on wealth, savings and debt.

Sources of wealth

Aggregate data on the wealth of the household sector compiled in the ONS National Accounts indicate that of total assets of £5,740 billion in 2002, over 50 per cent was held in the form of non-financial assets, primarily housing. Even when account is taken of the loans outstanding on the purchase of housing, this form of wealth has shown strong growth between 1991 and 2002. This reflects the buoyant state of the housing market, as well as the continued growth in the number of owner-occupied dwellings (see Chapter 5: Living standards).

The second most important element of household wealth is financial assets held in life assurance and pension funds, amounting to £1,377 billion in 2002. Having grown strongly in real terms during the 1990s, this element of household wealth fell by 21 per cent in real terms between 2000 and 2002, reflecting the fall in stock market values over this period. The Income section above drew attention to the fact that occupational and private pensions are important determinants of where older people appear in the income distribution, and so one of the government's OfA indicators is the proportion of working age people contributing to a non-state pension. In 2002/03, the FRS found that 44 per cent were doing so in Great Britain, with substantially more men (46 per cent) than women (38 per cent) making contributions.

Around three in five men aged between 35 and 54 had entitlement to a non-state pension in the United Kingdom in 2002/03, compared with less than half of women of the same age (Table 4.10). Except in the youngest age group where very few people have personal pensions, men are twice as likely as women to own them. The gap between men and women's

Table 4.10

Ownership of occupational and personal pensions: working age adults by age[1] and sex, 2002/03

United Kingdom   Percentages

	Men						All men of working age	Women					All women of working age
	16–24	25–34	35–44	45–54	55–59	60–64		16–24	25–34	35–44	45–54	55–59	
Personal pension	2	12	19	20	17	13	14	1	6	8	9	8	7
Occupational pension	11	34	44	42	31	15	33	13	33	37	37	25	31
Any non-state pension	13	46	62	61	47	28	46	14	40	45	45	32	38

1 Age at last birthday.

Source: Family Resources Survey, Department for Work and Pensions

ownership of occupational pensions is not as great; indeed for the under 35s the proportions are very similar. There is no clear relationship between ownership of an occupational pension and having other financial savings: the same proportion of working age adults with an occupational pension were living in families with no savings as were living in families with savings of over £20,000. The same is true of personal pensions.

Savings

Forms of wealth that might most naturally be thought of as 'savings', for example, savings accounts, stocks and shares, form a relatively small part of the total assets of the household sector: £1,194 billion in 2002, or about a fifth of the total. In 2002/03 the FRS showed that a third of individuals were living in families with no savings in these forms, and this proportion has scarcely changed over the past nine years. The lower the income of the household, the more likely an individual is to live in a family with no savings. Even in the top quintile group, one in eight individuals had no family savings, though one in four had savings of £20,000 or more.

It is not surprising that pensioner households are the most likely to have savings of £20,000 or more because they may have had the opportunity to build up their savings over their working lives. However, among pensioner families there is polarisation of the savings distribution: although a fifth have savings of £20,000 or more, a quarter have no savings at all and a further quarter have savings of less than £3,000.

Apart from income and age, other factors are important too. Households headed by a Black/Black British or Asian/Asian British person are nearly twice as likely as households overall to have no savings (Table 4.11). However, among Asian/Asian British households, those headed by someone of Indian origin

are more likely to have savings than are those of Pakistani/Bangladeshi origin.

Research using the BHPS shows that in 2000, 43 per cent of adults in Great Britain said that they were saving money out of their regular income.[8] A further 30 per cent said that they regularly put money aside and about the same proportion were saving for the long term (27 per cent). Of all those who saved, 41 per cent said that the money was not earmarked for any particular purpose. The most common specific purpose was for holidays (22 per cent), followed by saving for old age (nine per cent), house purchase (five per cent) and special events (five per cent).

People's subjective assessment of their financial situation had by far the greatest impact on regular saving, and also on long-term saving. Thus 43 per cent of people who said they were living comfortably saved regularly, but the proportion declined with the degree of economic hardship felt so that only three per cent of those who were finding it very difficult to cope saved regularly (Figure 4.12). This is a stronger relationship than with current income or current employment status, even though as might be expected, people with low incomes and those not in work were the least likely to be saving regularly. People paying into or receiving a non-state pension were both more likely to save than those without one, and to save larger sums of money. This effect persisted even when other factors such as income and employment status were controlled for.

Borrowing and debt

Having no savings is an important component of exclusion not just because savings can provide a flow of current income but because they enable people to smooth their expenditure over a period of time, thus helping them to cope with unexpected

Table **4.11**

Household savings: by ethnic group of head of household, 2002/03

United Kingdom

Percentages

	No savings	Less than £1,500	£1,500 but less than £10,000	£10,000 but less than £20,000	£20,000 or more	All households (=100%, thousands)
White	32	21	26	9	13	27,112
Mixed	46	25	..	..	..	137
Asian or Asian British	60	15	16	5	5	699
Black or Black British	63	18	15	..	..	456
Chinese or Other Ethnic Group	50	18	19	..	..	306
All households	33	20	25	8	13	28,710

Source: Family Resources Survey, Department for Work and Pensions

Figure **4.12**

Regular saving: by self-assessment of financial situation, 2000

Great Britain

Percentages

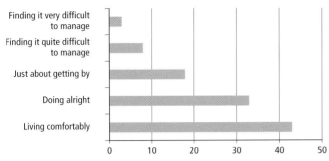

Source: Department for Work and Pensions from the British Household Panel Survey, Institute for Social and Economic Research

demands on their income without getting into financial difficulties. Without the cushion of savings, people may have to borrow money and thus get into debt. For many people, the debt can be serviced in the short term, i.e. the interest payments can be afforded, and the capital sum borrowed can be repaid in the longer term. However, if the ratio of debt to current income is high then there may be cause for concern. The distinction is often made between secured and unsecured debt: secured borrowing is through mortgages on the purchase of dwellings, whereas unsecured debt is acquired through personal loans, overdrafts and credit cards. While the aggregate stock of unsecured debt (£164 billion at the end of June 2003) is small in relation to the stock of mortgage debt (£714 billion) and both types have been growing rapidly in recent years,[9] it is unsecured borrowing that causes most concern. (Note that the aggregate estimate of unsecured debt includes credit used temporarily to make transactions, for example using credit cards even if the balance is paid off at the end of each month; however, in the household survey data used below this type of very short-term borrowing is excluded).

Survey research commissioned by the Bank of England indicated that in October 2003, about a third of adults had some form of unsecured debt over and above that which they expected to pay off at the end of the month (Table 4.13). This proportion was much the same as indicated by estimates from the BHPS for 1995 and 2000, so it would appear that the growth in unsecured debt is not driven by an increase in the number of debtors. Around 54 per cent of adults aged 25 to 34 had some unsecured debt, the highest rate of any age group. This age group also had the highest proportion of debtors reporting that their debt was a heavy burden, despite the fact that their debt to income ratio was not very different from other age groups. However, their finances are likely to be

Table **4.13**

Characteristics of adults with unsecured debt: by age, 2003

United Kingdom

Age group	Proportion with unsecured debt (percentages)	Mean debt to income ratio	Proportion of debtors reporting debt to be a heavy burden (percentages)
15–24	33	0.45	11
25–34	54	0.19	13
35–44	50	0.18	10
45–54	39	0.19	9
55–64	26	0.13	5
65 and over	7	0.75	5
All adults	34	0.24	10

Source: Bank of England, commissioned from NMG Research

under particular strain at a stage in their life when they are taking on mortgage borrowing and starting families.

The average amount owed by debtors in October 2003 was £3,500, but there was wide variation in the amounts owed. Most debtors owed relatively small amounts: 43 per cent owed less than £1,000 and 64 per cent owed less than £3,000. However, 13 per cent owed £10,000 or more, implying that a large proportion of unsecured debt is concentrated among relatively few people. The survey found that 10 per cent of individuals considered their unsecured debt to be a heavy burden, and again this proportion is similar to that reported in the BHPS data for 1995 and 2000.

The debt to income ratio of 0.45 for those aged 15 to 24 is the highest of the age groups shown in Table 4.13 (apart from the 65 and over age group who in any case have a very low participation rate and may be aiming to repay their debts from assets rather than income). This ratio will be influenced by the high proportion of students who are financing their studies in part through student loans. In the academic year 2002/03, nearly half the total income of undergraduate students aged under 25 came from student loans, hardship loans and Access/Hardship scheme funds, and over 80 per cent of students had some income from these sources.[10] By the end of the academic year, the majority (87 per cent) were in debt, and the average debt over all students was just under £5,500. Factors associated with having high amounts of debt were living in rented accommodation not owned by their university and coming from the lower social classes. The latter group of students were the most reliant on student loans but also borrowed more than the average amount of commercial credit and were the least likely to have any savings to offset against their debts or to get financial help from their families. Final year students expected to leave with an average debt of £8,666, and half anticipated leaving with debts of over £9,670. Data compiled by the Students Loans Company indicate that at the end of the financial year 2002/03, there were 2.6 million people with Student Loan borrowing, of whom 1.5 million borrowers had accounts on which repayments were, or were due, to be made.[11] Of these 1.5 million, 55 per cent, were up-to-date or ahead with their repayments, while 10 per cent owed two or more months' repayment. A further 37 per cent had deferred repayments.

Survey research carried out in 2002 on behalf of the Department of Trade and Industry's Task Force on Overindebtedness explored the causes, extent and effect of indebtedness.[12] This showed that access to credit was widespread, with three quarters of households having credit facilities of some kind. However, many did not use them and about half of households had credit commitments. Most used credit modestly and only a small minority were heavy credit users: seven per cent had four or more credit commitments, and five per cent were spending a quarter or more of their gross income on consumer credit payments. Overall, about a quarter of households reported that they had been in financial difficulties in the last 12 months. Despite low levels of unemployment, the largest single cause of these difficulties was job loss, though they were also strongly associated with setting up a home and having a family. The arrival of a new baby increased the risk, as did relationship breakdown. It appeared that the most common response when people have difficulty keeping up repayments is to re-finance rather than to claim on payment protection insurance or to seek advice from a free money advice service.

Conclusion

Over the last 30 years, the United Kingdom has seen considerable economic growth and this has been reflected in an increase in both household income and wealth. However, people have not necessarily benefited equally from these improvements. Although incomes have risen, the distribution of income is still far from equal and over the last 30 years has widened. Ownership of wealth is even more concentrated at the top of the distribution than is income, even though it is less polarised than a century ago. The use of credit has become widespread and though most people manage their debts sensibly, a small minority get into difficulties. Chapter 5

explores how these changes have been translated into changes in living standards.

References

1. Goodman S and Shephard A (2002), *Inequality and living standards in Great Britain: some facts*, Institute for Fiscal Studies, Briefing Note no. 19, *http://www.ifs.org.uk/ inequality/bn19.pdf*

2. Brewer M, Goodman A, Myck M, Shaw J and Shephard A (2004), *Poverty and Inequality in Britain: 2004*, Institute for Fiscal Studies, Commentary no. 96, *http://www.ifs.org.uk/ inequality/comm96.pdf*

3. Department for Work and Pensions (2003), *Measuring Child Poverty*, *http://www.dwp.gov.uk/consultations/consult/ 2003/childpov/final.pdf* See also DWP research showing the link between persistent low income and material deprivation - Berthoud R, Bryan M and Bardasi E, *The Dynamics of Deprivation*, DWP Research Report (forthcoming)

4. Hillyard P, Kelly G, McLaughlin E, Patsios D and Tomlinson M (2003), *Bare Necessities. Poverty and Social Exclusion in Northern Ireland: key findings*, Democratic Dialogue, Report 16, October 2003, *http://www.democraticdialogue.org/ PSEtsvqxf.pdf*

5. The effects of taxes and benefits on household income, 2002–03, Office for National Statistics (2004) *Economic Trends* 607, June 2004, 39–83

6. Dearden L, Machin S and Reed H (1997), Intergenerational mobility in Britain, *Economic Journal*, 107 (January), 47–66

7. Royal Commission on the Distribution of Income and Wealth 1975, quoted in A B Atkinson and A J Harrison, *Distribution of personal wealth in Britain*, Cambridge University Press 1978, Table 6.1

8. McKay S and Kempson E (2003) *Savings and life events*, Department for Work and Pensions, Research Report 194, *http://www.dwp.gov.uk/asd/asd5/rports2003-2004/ rrep194.asp*

9. Office for National Statistics (2004), *Social Trends* 34, Table 5.25, *http://www.statistics.gov.uk/socialtrends*

10.Callender C and Wilkinson D (2003) 2002/03 *Student Income and Expenditure Survey*: Student's income, expenditure and debt in 2002/03 and changes since 1998/ 99, London South Bank University/Policy Studies Institute, Department for Education and Skills, Research Report 487, *http://www.dfes.gov.uk/research/data/uploadfiles/ RR487.pdf*

11.Department for Education and Skills (2003), *Student Support: Statistics of Student Loans for Higher Education in the United Kingdom* – Financial year 2002/03 and Academic year 2002/03, SFR 32/2003, *http://www.dfes.gov.uk/ rsgateway/DB/SFR/s000428/SFR32-2003.pdf*

12.Kempson E (2002) *Over-indebtedness in Britain*, A Report to the Department of Trade and Industry, University of Bristol Personal Finance Research Centre, September 2002, *http://www.dti.gov.uk/ccp/topics1/overindebtedness.htm*

Further reading

Bromley C (2003) Has Britain become immune to inequality? In *British Social Attitudes,* National Centre for Social Research

Living Standards

Paul Haezewindt and Valerie Christian

Chapter 5

Introduction

Living standards reflect the different lifestyles and quality of life that people experience and have implications for people's happiness and well being, health and social participation. Inequalities in living standards describe the day to day circumstances and living conditions in which different groups of people live, from the most advantaged to the most disadvantaged groups, such as rough sleepers. A wide range of factors, such as labour market participation or income and wealth (which are examined in Chapters 3 and 4) influence living standards. However, this chapter refers solely to people's material circumstances, such as their access to decent housing, quality of the local environment (including incidence of anti-social behaviour and crime), and access to transport and services. These issues highlight the real life experiences of inequality and demonstrate what it means to be disadvantaged or live in a deprived area.

Expenditure and material resources

Income is not always a reliable guide to living standards. Studies repeatedly show only modest levels of correlation between current income, and indicators of lifestyle or deprivation. As Table 4.4 in the previous chapter shows, the proportion of people who said their household's income allowed them to 'live comfortably' increased by 15 percentage points to 39 per cent between 1984 and 2002. Nevertheless, there remain differences in households' abilities to afford the various goods and services which are widely regarded as necessary to enjoy an acceptable standard of living, and to enable participation in social customs and activities. The proportions of total spending by rich and poor households on different categories of goods, services, and consumer durables are also discussed in an effort to understand how patterns of spending relate to the amount of money a household has to spend.

Access to necessities

The Breadline Britain surveys of 1983 and 1990 pioneered the approach to measuring material deprivation in terms of access to those items that the public perceives to be 'necessities'; in other words, items that someone should not have to do without because they could not afford them. In 1999 this method was extended by the Poverty and Social Exclusion Survey.[1]

People's perceptions of what constituted necessities in 1999 showed a high degree of agreement, although some differences between more and less affluent groups, between men and women, and between adults above and below 30 years of age were noted. The items chosen as necessities by a majority of respondents were not restricted to basic material needs such as nutrition, clothes and shelter. Indeed, activities such as celebrating Christmas or birthdays, visiting friends or family in hospital, and having a hobby or leisure activity, were all seen as necessities by more than three quarters of the British population.

Figure 5.1 shows the percentages of households in Great Britain lacking selected necessities in 1983, 1990 and 1999 because they were unable to afford them. More than a quarter of households in 1999 could not afford even small monthly savings (of £10) for a rainy day or retirement (see also Figure 4.12 in Chapter 4), with at least a tenth of households not able to afford to maintain their home's decoration, or to have contents insurance. These proportions changed little over the period.

Figure **5.1**

Households without access to selected goods, services or activities because they cannot afford them

Great Britain

Percentages

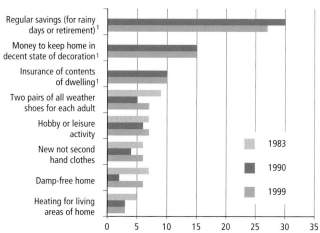

1 Not asked in 1983.

Source: Breadline Britain (1983, 1990); Poverty and Social Exclusion Survey (1999)

Around a fifth of children in Great Britain lived in low-income households in 2002/03 (see page 46), and the Government's stated aim is to eradicate child poverty in the United Kingdom within a generation. However, the impacts of inequality and poverty on children's lives are not fully explained by the level of their household's income for various reasons. Data suggests, for example, that parents in many poor households try to protect their children from being deprived of necessities, by ensuring that they have a high priority when deciding how to spend their money.[1]

Nevertheless, families spent less money on leisure activities than on most other expenditure items, and this may be due to giving a lower priority to leisure compared with food, clothing, or home appliances. This is particularly true of lone-parent families, who were less able to afford leisure activities than were couple families. Figure 5.2 shows that nearly three fifths of lone-parent families were unable to afford a week's holiday not staying with relatives, and that two fifths did not have money for trips, outings, or for presents. This contrasted most sharply with couple families where special occasions are almost always celebrated with presents, and where toys and sports gear were available for most children.

Figure **5.2**

Children in households unable to afford selected leisure activities, 2002

Great Britain

Percentages

Source: Family and Children Study, Department for Work and Pensions

Patterns of expenditure

A household's level of expenditure is directly related to its income level. Households with lower incomes spend less on all categories of goods and services when compared with higher income households. At the same time, lower income households often spend larger proportions of their total income on the most essential commodities such as food, electricity and gas, while spending smaller proportions on others. This tendency for lower income households to spend higher proportions of their total expenditure on essentials has persisted despite the fact that increases in disposable incomes over the past 20 years have resulted in both low and high income households devoting larger proportions of their expenditure to non-essentials such as spending abroad, and recreation and culture. In 2002/03 results from the Expenditure and Food Survey (EFS) show that households in the United Kingdom with the lowest incomes still spent only around £17 a week on recreation and culture, compared with £116 by households with the highest incomes. However, these very different levels of spending respectively accounted for similar

proportions (12 and 13 per cent) of the households' overall weekly expenditure.

Figure 5.3 shows proportions of weekly spending on selected categories of goods and services by the lowest and highest 10 percentile (decile) income groups of households in the United Kingdom. The income data here are not adjusted (equivalised) to account for the fact that different household compositions require different levels of income to achieve the same standard of living. The lowest income group of households spent around £40 (almost a third) of their weekly expenditure on essential items such as food and non-alcoholic drink, and fuel and power for the home. In comparison, households in the top income group spent more than three times this amount (around £125 per week) on these items, although this represents less than a fifth of their total weekly expenditure.

Figure **5.3**

Weekly household expenditure for selected goods and services as a proportion of total expenditure in the lowest and highest gross income groups[1], 2002/03

United Kingdom

Percentages

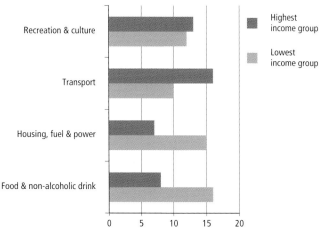

1 Households in the lowest 10th percentile group and highest 10th percentile group.

Source: Expenditure and Food Survey, Office for National Statistics

Conversely, households in the highest income group spent about £140 (almost 16 per cent) of their weekly outgoings on transport, compared with households in the lowest decile group who spent less than £15 (about 10 per cent) of their weekly expenditure on this. Lower levels of car ownership (see Figure 5.12) largely explain the relatively small proportions spent on transport by the lowest income group. Lone parents with dependent children and single pensioner households were most likely to fall into this group.

Access to goods and services

Access to goods and services at home are generally related to a household's disposable income. Figure 5.4 compares selected goods and services available in some of the lowest income households in Great Britain in 2001/02, with that in households with incomes exceeding £1,000 per week. In all cases, higher proportions of more affluent households had access to these goods and services. There are, however, differences between access to more established items that have been available for several decades and those that only became available in the early to mid-1990s.

Figure **5.4**

Access to selected consumer goods and services: by highest and lowest total weekly disposable household income[1], 2001/02

Great Britain

Percentages

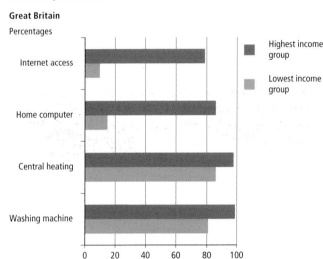

1 Income adjusted for household size and composition by means of equivalence scales. Lowest income group: £100 to less than £200 weekly income. Highest income group: £1,000 or more weekly income.

Source: Family Resources Survey, Department for Work and Pensions

More established goods like washing machines and central heating, once regarded as luxuries, have become necessities and are found in a large majority of households across all income groups and household types. It is important to highlight differences in household ownership of these more common items, as a household is likely to have an increased perception of disadvantage if it lacks these items which are available to most other households.

Almost all (99 per cent) of households with children have washing machines. Such high levels are likely to be explained by the need to deal with large amounts of washing. However, five per cent of lone-parent households with one dependent child did not have a washing machine in 2001/02. Lone-parent households with more than one child were as likely to have washing machines as households with couple parents.

On average, 91 per cent of all households in Great Britain had central heating in their homes in 2001/02. However, having

central heating can vary by household type. The Government launched the UK Fuel Strategy in 2001, aimed at assisting provision to those in social housing, and to vulnerable groups. For example, single pensioner households remain the least likely to have central heating, despite being one of the groups most vulnerable to the effects of cold indoor temperatures.[2] Furthermore, even though many older people spend more than 10 per cent of their incomes on fuel, many fail to achieve recommended safe levels of warmth.

In 2001, people aged 60 years or above living alone made up the largest proportion (40 per cent) of those with fuel costs in excess of 10 per cent of total household income.[3] This compares with an average fuel bill across all households of around 3.5 per cent of total household income.[4] The Government has stated an aim to end excessive household spending on fuel by 2010, and to enable everyone to afford to keep warm in his or her home.

Cars and other vehicles for personal use represent another category of established consumer durables that still shows low levels of access among lower income groups (see Figure 5.12 and Table 5.13).

Access to information technology

One of the methods by which the Government hopes to raise standards in education, and so increase peoples' chances of gaining employment, is through the use of computers and the Internet. One way of doing this is to provide access at school. The Department for Education and Skills' Survey of Information and Communications Technology in 2003, found that more than 99 per cent of all maintained primary and secondary schools in England had access to computers, the majority of which were connected to the Internet. Nevertheless, limited resources may still result in several students having to share access to one terminal. There was, for example, one computer for every eight children in maintained primary schools, and one for every five children in maintained secondary schools in 2003.

Limited availability of school computers may be compensated for by their use at home. As in schools, access to home computers and the Internet has also increased rapidly in recent years. Regardless of social class, children's educational needs were a reason over 80 per cent of parents bought a home computer, with over a half of parents giving children's needs as the main reason.[5] Indeed, according to the Family Resources Survey (FRS), half of all households in Great Britain in 2001/02 had a home computer, while two fifths had access to the Internet. These overall figures, however, mask much variability. Less than a third of single parent households had access at home to either computers or the Internet in 2001/02, while at least two thirds of couple households with children did. Financial barriers were mentioned by 63 per cent of respondents as the main factor preventing parents who did not have a computer at home from buying one.[5] Overall, less than 20 per cent of households with some of the lowest incomes had access to home computers in 2001/02, compared with almost 90 per cent of households with the highest incomes (Figure 5.4).

Apart from children's educational needs, the Internet is also increasingly accessed for a variety of services targeting adult users. For example, supermarket and other retail shopping, travel bookings, and banking services, can be done using the Internet. These services may be more convenient for the consumer, and are often offered at competitive prices. In addition, the Government has stated a commitment to make all Government services available on the Internet by 2005. Some of those already available include job advertisements, benefit advice, and registration of vital statistics such as marriages, births and deaths.

Pensioner households and single person households of working age are the least likely to have computer or Internet access at home, with Internet access in such households ranging from 16 per cent to 40 per cent respectively. Of all groups, older people were the least likely to use the Internet, despite the proportion of users aged 55 to 64 having greatly increased since July 2000 (when Internet data were first collected on the Omnibus Survey) when 33 per cent had accessed the Internet. According to NS Omnibus Survey, by April 2004 just 48 per cent of this group in Great Britain had used the Internet, compared with 92 per cent of 16 to 24 year olds. People aged 55 or above are also more likely to state they did not want, did not need, or had no interest in the Internet as their reason for non-use. Conversely, the FRS shows that in 2001/02 households with working-age couples, three or more adults, and most of those with children, enjoyed levels of access to either computers or the Internet ranging from more than 50 per cent to over 80 per cent.

Housing and homelessness

Having adequate shelter is a necessity for life. A person's home and housing conditions can have a major impact upon their health and well-being. For the majority of households, housing costs including fuel and power constitute a large share of weekly expenditure (see Figure 5.3). For those who own their homes housing usually represents the most important investment that they will make and forms over half the value of total household wealth. Those who are homeless and those sleeping rough on the streets constitute some of the poorest, most disadvantaged and socially excluded members of society.

Housing tenure

Over the past thirty years, the proportion of households in Great Britain owning their own home has increased considerably. According to estimates from the General Household Survey (GHS) the proportion owning their property, either outright or with a mortgage, has increased from 49 per cent in 1971 to 69 per cent in 2002. In the same period, the proportion of households renting socially from local authorities and housing associations decreased from 32 to 20 per cent, and the proportion of households renting from the private sector fell from 20 to 11 per cent. The decline in the proportion of privately rented households ended in the late 1980s following the 1988 Housing Act, which abolished rent control for new tenancies. Since then there has been no further decline.

Home ownership is strongly linked to income and employment status. Results from the Disadvantaged Households Supplement to the GHS in 2000[6] showed that 47 per cent of households in Great Britain with a gross weekly income of less than £250 owned their own homes, compared with 81 per cent of all other households. Low rates of home ownership were also found in workless households (35 per cent) and households dependent on state benefits (25 per cent). As may be expected, given the links between employment, income and education levels, people with the highest qualifications were more likely to own their homes than those with lower or no qualifications. According to the Labour Force Survey in 2001 four fifths of households in the United Kingdom headed by someone with a higher educational qualification or a degree owned their home compared with half of households headed by someone with no qualifications. Other households less likely to own their homes included lone parents with dependent children (34 per cent) and households where all adults had a long-term health problem (48 per cent). Age was also an important factor in home ownership. In 2002 the proportion of owner occupiers in Great Britain rose steadily with age from 25 per cent of those aged under 25 to 81 per cent of those aged 60 to 64. The proportion of home owners fell gradually for older people to 63 per cent for those aged over 80, although the proportion of people who owned their homes outright peaked for those aged 65 and over as most older people have paid off their mortgages.

Despite a trend for greater home ownership, the number of first-time buyers has decreased in recent years. The Survey of Mortgage Lenders shows that in the United Kingdom the proportion of first-time buyers, out of all buyers, has fallen from 54 per cent in 1994 to 22 per cent in 2003, and the average age of first-time buyers has increased from 30 in 1974 to 31 in 2003. A major barrier for first-time buyers and those wanting to move up the property ladder has been the rapid increase in property prices over the past twenty years. In 2003 the average (cash) property price in the United Kingdom was £155,600, over six times the cost in 1982 (£23,600) (Figure 5.5). There are also considerable regional variations, with prices highest in London and the South East and lowest in Northern Ireland, the North East and Scotland.

Figure **5.5**

Simple average property prices

United Kingdom

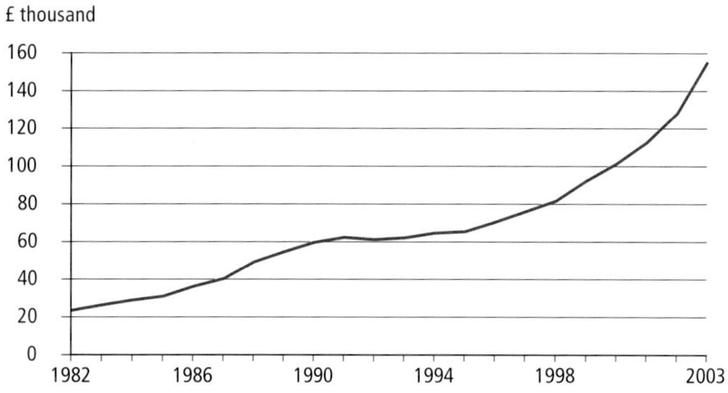

£ thousand

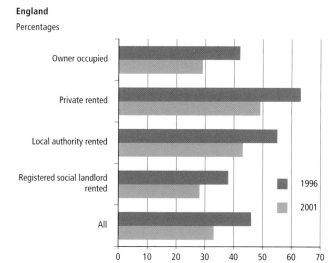

Source: Office of the Deputy Prime Minister

Although home ownership is an important form of wealth, it does not necessarily follow that those who own their homes have high incomes. Research using the 1999 Poverty and Social Exclusion Survey highlighted that many people in Great Britain living in poverty, defined as not being able to afford two or more socially defined necessities, owned their own homes.[7] Research showed that although the poverty rate in the owner-occupied sector was lower than for other tenures, the relative size of the sector meant that 50 per cent of those living in poverty were either outright owners (18 per cent) or were paying towards a mortgage (32 per cent). By this measure, owner occupation was the most common tenure for people living in poverty, compared with those living in socially rented housing (41 per cent) or tenants in the private sector (nine per cent). Many of the owner occupiers living in poverty are pensioners, who own their home outright (not paying a mortgage).

Housing conditions

According to the English House Condition Survey (EHCS) in 2001 there were 21.1 million dwellings in England. Thirty three per cent of dwellings were found to be in a non-decent state, defined as property being unfit, in disrepair, in need of modernisation or providing insufficient thermal comfort (Figure 5.6). The proportion of non-decent dwellings had fallen from 46 per cent in 1996. In 2001 almost half of all privately rented dwellings were considered non-decent (49 per cent). A high proportion of local authority housing was also found to be

non-decent (43 per cent), while less than a third of owner occupied (29 per cent) and registered social landlord (28 per cent) dwellings were below this standard. The proportion of dwellings in a non-decent state has fallen for all tenure types since 1996. Households where people lived alone, minority ethnic households, and households where no one was in full-time employment were also more likely to have non-decent housing than the general population.

Figure **5.6**

Non-decent[1] homes: by tenure[2]

England

Percentages

1 Non-decent homes are defined as homes being unfit, in disrepair, in need of modernisation or provide insufficient thermal comfort.
2 Registered social landlord: includes all households living in the property of registered housing associations.

Source: English House Condition Survey, Office of the Deputy Prime Minister

Overcrowding and under-occupancy are other indicators of housing standards. The bedroom standard measures the number of bedrooms available in a property against the number required given the household's size and composition (see Appendix, Part 5: Bedroom standard). In 2002/03 the Survey of English Housing (SEH) found that two per cent of households in England lived in dwellings that were below the bedroom standard and defined as overcrowded, while 36 per cent of households had two or more bedrooms above the standard and were under-occupied. Overcrowding was most common in rented accommodation from the private or social sectors (five per cent each), rather than in owner-occupied housing (one per cent). Forty five per cent of owner-occupied households lived in dwellings considered as under-occupied, compared with 13 per cent of households living in the social sector and 17 per cent living in private sector dwellings. In 2001 the EHCS found that retired households and people living alone had the most living space. Living space, defined as average floor space divided by the number of people in a household, was lowest among those living in large households and households with children. It impacts disproportionately on minority ethnic households, particularly Pakistani and Bangladeshi households who were least likely to have sufficient bedrooms to meet their needs because suitably sized homes were either unavailable or unaffordable.

Along with the recent trend for more people to own their homes in recent years, the number of households that own a second home has also increased. The SEH recorded that the number of households in England with a second home (anywhere) increased by 37 per cent from 329,000 households in 1994/95 to 450,000 in 2002/03.

Homelessness

The number of people becoming homeless has also increased over time. According to the Office of the Deputy Prime Minister (ODPM) the number of households in England which have applied for housing assistance from local authorities and have been classified as homeless has increased from 164,620 in 1997/98 to 201,550 in 2002/03. People may experience homelessness or be at risk of becoming homeless for a variety of reasons. Risk factors include a loss of income through redundancy, relationship breakdown (with parents, a partner or friends), traumatic events such as a fire or flood, eviction, and drug, alcohol and mental health problems. Many homeless people turn to friends and relatives for somewhere to live or move into temporary accommodation such as hostels or bed and breakfast hotels. Others, however, turn to local authorities for help and a small proportion sleep rough on the street.

Under existing homeless legislation, local housing authorities have a statutory duty to provide advice and assistance to anyone who requests help with their housing. Local authorities must provide suitable accommodation for homeless applicants who are eligible for assistance and who have a priority need (the main housing duty). In England almost half (137,220) of the 298,490 decisions made in 2003 were accepted as unintentionally homeless and in priority need. Homelessness acceptances for other countries in the United Kingdom in 2002/03, ranged from 26,930 in Scotland to 8,580 in Northern Ireland and 6,965 in Wales. In England 51 per cent of households accepted had a dependent child and 10 per cent of acceptances were for households with a pregnant woman in 2003. Other acceptances included applicants who were vulnerable because of mental illness (nine per cent), domestic violence (five per cent), physical handicap (five per cent), or were young (eight per cent) or old (three per cent).

For households accepted as homeless by English local authorities in 2003, the main reason for the loss of last settled home – for over a third of households – was that parents, relatives or friends were no longer able or willing to

accommodate them (Figure 5.7). In contrast, a fifth of households became homeless as a result of a relationship breakdown with a partner, two thirds of which involved violence. Another fifth resulted from the end or loss of private rented or tied accommodation. Three per cent resulted from rent or mortgage arrears. However, mortgage arrears was a much more common reason for statutory homelessness in the early 1990s (11 per cent in 1991). Over the last 30 years, the number of properties repossessed in the United Kingdom peaked at 75,540 in 1991, from a low of 1,220 in 1973, and has since fallen gradually to 7,630 in 2003.

Figure **5.7**

Households accepted as homeless by local authorities: by main reason for loss of last settled home

England

Percentages

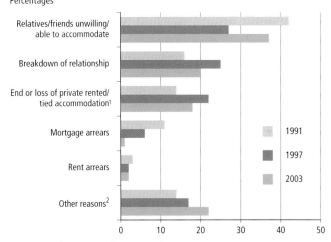

1 Mainly the ending of an assured tenancy.
2 Includes households leaving an institution (such as hospital, prison or a residential home), and those returning from abroad, sleeping rough or in hostels, or made homeless by an emergency such as fire or flooding.

Source: Office of the Deputy Prime Minister

Shortages of affordable housing in many areas means that many homeless people must be housed for long periods in temporary accommodation until a settled home is found. According to the ODPM, at the end of December 2003 half of households were temporarily housed in private sector accommodation (either leased by social landlords or directly rented), 11 per cent were in hostels/womens refuges and nine per cent in bed and breakfast hotels. Nearly a third were in other types of accommodation, which included local authority owned stock and that owned by registered social landlords. Temporary accommodation can often be insecure and inadequate for the needs of homeless people, particularly for families with children, and households can sometimes be located far away from their original home and support networks. In March 2002 the Government set up the Homelessness Directorate responsible for tackling homelessness, and set a target to end the use of bed and breakfast accommodation by March 2004 for families with dependent children, except in short-term emergencies, and even then for no longer than six weeks in total. At the end of March 2004 there had been a 99 per cent reduction in the use of bed and breakfast type accommodation by local authorities for more than six weeks for families with dependent children.

Many people live in temporary accommodation throughout England, but it is much more prevalent in London than any other region (Figure 5.8). At the end of December 2003, around 60 per cent of households in temporary accommodation lived in London. Overall, the number of people living in temporary accommodation grew in the late 1980s and early 1990s from 21,000 at the end of December 1986 to a peak of 66,000 at the end of September 1992. The number fell during the early to mid-1990s but has since more than doubled from 41,250 at the end of March 1997 to 95,000 at the end of December 2003. Five and a half times more households were in temporary accommodation in 2003 than 1986.

Rough sleepers are a small subset of homeless people, with around 500 estimated (in June 2003) to sleep on the streets in England each night. By definition rough sleepers are hard to keep track of and measure since they can sometimes refuse to co-operate with surveys and can be missed if they sleep in inaccessible places. Also, people seen begging, drinking and those apparently living on the streets during the day can influence public perceptions of the number of rough sleepers. However, many of these people do have somewhere to stay and do not sleep rough.[8] Estimates from the ODPM suggest that the number of rough sleepers have declined in recent years. The key government target to reduce the number of rough sleepers by at least two thirds compared with the figure

in 1998 was reached in 2001 and has since been sustained and reduced further. In 2003 the majority of rough sleepers in England could be found in London. Other concentrations of rough sleepers could also be found in Leeds, Liverpool, Exeter, Birmingham and Bristol.

Research shows that many rough sleepers share similar characteristics. Ninety five per cent of rough sleepers are White, 90 per cent are male and 75 per cent are aged over 25.[9] Between 25 and 33 per cent of rough sleepers have been in local authority care, around 50 per cent have been in prison or a remand centre at some time, and 20 to 25 per cent have been in the Armed Forces at some stage. Rough sleepers are less likely to have any qualifications than the general population, and are disproportionately likely to have missed school through truancy and/or exclusion.[8]

Very few rough sleepers do so by choice. The main reason given for the first incidence of rough sleeping is a relationship breakdown, either with parents or a partner. Other reasons include eviction, redundancy and mental illness. Around 30 to 50 per cent of rough sleepers suffer from a mental illness, and the majority of those people (88 per cent) had mental health problems before they became homeless.[8] Those sleeping rough on the streets have a high risk of illness, premature death, and are particularly vulnerable to crime, drug and alcohol abuse. Research indicates that rough sleepers have a life expectancy of only 42 years.[9] They often suffer from poor physical health, are four times more likely to die from unnatural causes (such as accidents, assaults, and drugs or alcohol poisoning) and are 35 times more likely to commit suicide than the general population. Fifty per cent of rough sleepers are alcohol reliant and around 70 per cent misuse drugs. Drug problems are particularly prevalent among younger rough sleepers.

Figure **5.8**

Homeless households in temporary accommodation[1]

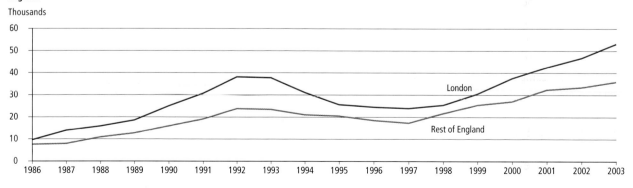

1 Households in accommodation arranged by local authorities in England under the homelessness provisions of the 1985 and 1996 Housing Acts. Data are for quarter 1 each year.

Source: Office of the Deputy Prime Minister

Local environment, anti-social behaviour and crime

The majority of people enjoy living in their local area. However, the type of neighbourhood where people live can have a major impact upon their enjoyment and living standards. Factors such as environmental problems and upkeep of the neighbourhood, local amenities, incidence of anti-social behaviour and crime all impact upon people's quality of life. Environmental problems include issues such as heavy traffic, problems caused by street parking, poor air quality, litter, vandalism, poor maintenance of gardens or public spaces, and neglected or boarded up buildings. Local amenities such as shops and health or leisure facilities contribute to people's living standards. Anti-social behaviour describes a range of problems such as noisy neighbours, abandoned cars, vandalism, graffiti and youth nuisance, and can create an environment which can encourage crime and fear of crime. The effect of this kind of behaviour, particularly when it is experienced day in and day out by individuals and communities will be greater than the individual events that comprise it. Cumulatively it can have a profound impact, undermining the quality of life of the wider community.

Enjoy living in local area

According to the social capital module of the GHS in 2000, 87 per cent of people in Great Britain enjoyed living in their local area.[10] However, enjoyment of the local area differed by people's social and economic circumstances, the type of area in which they lived and particularly by the level of deprivation experienced in that area. Sixty eight per cent of people in the 10 per cent most deprived wards enjoyed living in their local area, compared with 96 per cent of people in the 10 per cent least deprived wards (based on the 2000 ODPM Index of Multiple Deprivation).

Enjoyment of the local area also varied by tenure, access to transport, socio-economic group and employment status. Those who owned their homes (either outright or with a mortgage) and those renting from the private sector were more likely than those renting from the social sector to enjoy living in their local area. This was also true for people in households with cars compared with those without cars. Enjoyment was also higher among those from non-manual compared with manual socio-economic groups and those in employment rather than the unemployed.

Environmental problems

A variety of factors influence whether people enjoy living in an area or not. Local environmental and behavioural conditions contribute significantly to quality of life and can particularly affect certain groups of people and places. Results from the EHCS in 2001 found that the most common environmental problems for neighbourhoods related to heavy traffic and street parking, affecting 2.4 million dwellings in England. Just over 1 million dwellings were in neighbourhoods affected by neglected or poorly maintained buildings, gardens or public spaces, litter or dumping. Around half a million dwellings were found in neighbourhoods with serious problems of graffiti, vandalism and vacant or boarded up buildings. Neighbourhoods with environmental problems were also particularly likely to have high concentrations of non-decent dwellings. Environmental problems tended to be concentrated in city and other urban areas, and were particularly prevalent in the most deprived areas. Homes in the 10 per cent most deprived wards were eleven times more likely to be situated in a neighbourhood with serious environmental problems than homes in the 10 per cent least deprived wards (Figure 5.9).

Around half (49 per cent) of dwellings in neighbourhoods with environmental problems were owner occupied, 36 per cent were rented from the social sector, and 16 per cent rented from private landlords. Minority ethnic households were almost three times more likely to live in a neighbourhood with environmental problems than White households. Other high concentrations of people living in areas with environmental problems included those on a low income, the unemployed or economically inactive, lone parents, and people living alone or in shared households. Environmental problems in an area were

Figure

Dwellings in neighbourhoods with environmental problems[1]: by Index of Multiple Deprivation[2], 2001

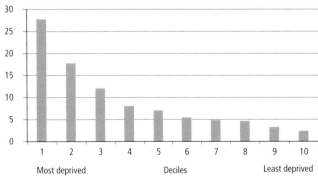

England
Percentages

1 Neighbourhoods assessed to have one or more of the following problems: over 10% of dwellings visually assessed to be seriously defective; vacant sites or derelict buildings; litter, rubbish or dumping; vandalism; graffiti or scruffy buildings, gardens or landscaping, neglected buildings; and very poor visual quality of local area.
2 Index of Multiple Deprivation; 2000 wards, ranked from top to bottom and divided into 10 equal percentile groups.

Source: English House Condition Survey, Office of the Deputy Prime Minister

closely associated with behavioural problems. People living in areas with environmental problems were more likely than those living elsewhere to identify where they live with behavioural problems such as anti-social behaviour and crime.

Anti-social behaviour

Twenty two per cent of people in England and Wales in 2002/03 perceived a high level of disorder in their local area. Figure 5.10 shows people's perceptions of different types of anti-social behaviour and disorder in their area. The single largest problem highlighted was vandalism and graffiti, which over a third of people perceived to be a very or fairly big problem. High proportions of people also considered teenagers hanging around on the streets, rubbish or litter, people using or dealing drugs and people being drunk or rowdy in public places a major problem. Anti-social behaviour was more likely to be considered a problem by those living in inner city areas, and in particular those living in council estates and those in areas where social cohesion was considered low. The Government in January 2003 set up the Home Office Anti-Social Behaviour Unit with a range of measures and initiatives to help tackle anti-social behaviour, including anti-social behaviour orders and acceptable behaviour contracts.

Crime and fear of crime

Environmental problems and anti-social behaviour can create an environment where crime and fear of crime can develop. These in turn affect people's quality of life in many ways and have implications for people's health and well-being and participation in social activities (see Chapter 7). According to the British Crime Survey (BCS) in 2002/03, 60 per cent of people in England and Wales reported that crime and fear of crime had a minimal impact upon their quality of life, 33 per cent cited a moderate impact and seven per cent considered their quality of life greatly affected. BCS results also suggested that crime had less of an effect on quality of life than fear of crime. This is possibly due to the fact that the likelihood of being a victim of crime is relatively low (over the course of a year) and tends to be concentrated in certain groups and areas, while the potential to be a victim is a possibility for all.[11]

Overall, 13 per cent of people felt very unsafe walking alone in their local area after dark and 21 per cent felt a bit unsafe. People were less likely to feel unsafe in their own home, with only one per cent saying they felt very unsafe and five per cent a bit unsafe. Fear of crime and concerns for personal safety vary considerably by factors such as sex, age, health, income, locality and prior victimisation. Women were more likely than men to feel very unsafe walking alone in their local area after dark: 21 per cent of women compared with five per cent of men. Concern about walking alone after dark also increased with age, and was particularly high for older women: 33 per cent of women aged 60 and over compared with 10 per cent of men in the same age range. People who considered themselves to be in poor health or to have a limiting illness or disability had higher levels of concern over crime than people in good health. A third of people with very bad or bad health felt very unsafe walking alone in the local area after dark, compared with a tenth of people in good or very good health.

Table **5.10**

Experience of anti-social behaviour: by type of area, 2002/03

England & Wales — Percentage saying very/fairly big problem in their area

	All adults	Inner-city	Urban	Rural	Council estate	Non-council estate
Vandalism, graffiti and other deliberate damage to property	35	54	37	20	51	32
Teenagers hanging around on streets	33	48	36	19	48	30
Rubbish or litter lying around	33	52	36	19	47	31
People using or dealing drugs	32	50	34	17	48	28
People being drunk or rowdy in public places	23	33	26	12	31	22
Noisy neighbours or loud parties	10	18	10	5	16	9
People being attacked/ harassed because of their race/colour	8	18	9	2	12	7

Source: British Crime Survey, Home Office

People with low household incomes were more likely to be concerned about crime and personal safety than those on higher incomes. As Figure 5.11 shows, those in households with annual incomes of less than £5,000 were more than four times more likely to feel unsafe walking alone in the dark than those with annual household incomes of £30,000 or more. This is likely to reflect the different types of area where people on different incomes tend to live. Fear of crime varies considerably across different types of locality, and is highest in inner city areas, council estates, areas with low levels of social cohesion, and areas with high levels of perceived disorder or anti-social behaviour. Fear of crime was also higher for people who had been a recent victim of crime. Victims of any crime in the BCS survey in the past year were more likely than non-victims to be very worried about crime and to feel very unsafe either walking alone in the dark or being at home alone at night.

Figure **5.11**

Proportion feeling very unsafe walking alone in area after dark: by gross annual household income, 2002/03

England & Wales

Percentages

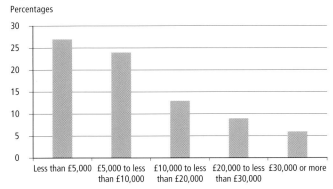

Source: British Crime Survey, Home Office

Transport and access to services

Over the past 50 years the distance travelled by people has increased considerably and society has become more organised around the car. According to the Department for Transport (DfT), the total distance travelled within Great Britain more than tripled between 1952 and 2002 to 746 billion passenger kilometres. For residents of Great Britain, the DfT's National Travel Survey (NTS) shows that the average trip length has increased by 48 per cent since the early 1970s from 7.5 kilometres in 1972/73 to 11.1 kilometres in 2002, and the overall distance travelled per person per year increased by 56 per cent from 7,200 to 11,200 kilometres. Transport constitutes a major expenditure for the majority of households. In 2002/03, in the United Kingdom the single largest weekly household expenditure on average was on transport (see Figure 5.3). Problems with access to transport and the location

of services can act as a major barrier to opportunities and services such as employment, education, health care, and can also obstruct participation in social, cultural and sporting activities. Often those most excluded from society have the poorest access to transport and therefore a lack of transport and poor access to services can further reinforce inequalities.

Access to transport

Since the early 1960s the car has been the dominant means of transport in Great Britain, and in 2002 accounted for 85 per cent of all passenger kilometres travelled. Findings from the NTS show that car ownership more than doubled during this period from 31 per cent of households owning a car in 1961 to 72 per cent in 2002. There has also been a steady rise in the proportion of households owning two or more cars from two per cent in 1961 to 29 per cent in 2002. However, there remains a significant proportion of households without access to a car, 28 per cent in 2002.

Car ownership is closely related to income, as well as to demographic factors such as sex, age, stage of life cycle, and the location in which people live. In 2002, 59 per cent of households in the lowest income quintile in Great Britain did not have access to a car, 35 per cent had one car and six per cent had two or more cars (Figure 5.12). For households in the highest income quintile, however, eight per cent did not own a car, while 43 per cent owned one car and 49 per cent owned two or more. Women were less likely than men to have access to a car or be able to drive, with fewer women having a driving licence compared with men. Twenty four per cent of women lived in a household without a car compared with 17 per cent of men in 2002, and 61 per cent of women had a driving licence in 2002 compared with 81 per cent of men. Younger people aged 17 to 20, and older people aged 70 and over,

Figure **5.12**

Household car ownership: by income quintile group, 2002

Great Britain

Percentages

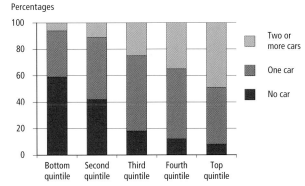

Source: National Travel Survey, Department for Transport

were less likely to have a driving licence than those aged between 21 and 69.

Table 5.13 shows differences in the rates of car ownership by household type. In 2001, single pensioners in Great Britain, who were most likely to be women, were the least likely to own a car, and were three times less likely than pensioner couples to have access to a car. High proportions of households without access to a car could also be found among lone parent and single person and student households. Non-pensioner couple households were most likely to have access to a car and couples with dependent or non-dependent children were more likely than those without to own a car. Couples with children, particularly those with non-dependent children, were the most likely to have two or more cars.

People living in rural areas were more likely to own a car than those living in more built-up areas. According to the NTS in 2002, rural households were much more likely to have access to a car than households in built-up London and other metropolitan areas. Car ownership in rural areas is often a necessity as sparsely populated areas tend to have less and infrequent public transport facilities and fewer local amenities than more densely populated areas. The Countryside Agency's Rural Services Survey in 2000 estimated that 29 per cent of rural settlements in England had no bus service and that many settlements did not have key services such as a doctors surgery (92 per cent), general food store (78 per cent), Post Office (74 per cent), or village shop (72 per cent).

People living in households without access to a car travel a shorter distance each year than those with access to a car, and also make fewer trips. Walking was the mode of transport most frequently used by those without access to a car, accounting for 50 per cent of trips in 2002, followed by the use of bus and coach services (21 per cent) (Figure 5.14). Lifts from friends or relatives were another important mode of transport for those without access to a car and mainly account for the 18 per cent of trips made by car by those people. The Disabled Persons Transport Advisory Committee (DiPTAC) highlighted that this was also the most common means of transport for disabled people. In contrast, 20 per cent of trips made by those with access to a car was by walking, 73 per cent by car and three per cent by bus and coach.

Barriers to transport and travel

Cost can be a major barrier to car ownership for those on low incomes. The EFS in 2002/03 estimated that the average amount spent on private motoring (including purchase, maintenance and fuel) in the United Kingdom was £50.70 a week compared with £8.50 spent on public transport fares and other costs. Public transport costs in the United Kingdom are

Table **5.13**

Number of cars per household[1]: by household composition, 2001

Great Britain			Percentages
	No car	One car	Two or more cars
One person			
Under state pension age	39	55	5
Over state pension age	69	30	1
All	53	43	3
One family and no others			
All pensioner	22	63	15
Couple family households[2]	8	41	51
No children	9	46	45
With dependent child(ren)[3]	7	40	53
Non-dependent child(ren) only	7	27	65
Lone parent households	43	46	12
With dependent child(ren)[3]	48	47	5
Non-dependent child(ren) only	33	43	24
All	15	45	40
Other households			
With dependent child(ren)[3]	22	38	39
All student	44	30	26
All pensioners	44	43	13
Other	25	35	40
All	26	37	37
All households	27	44	29

1 Includes any company car or van if available for private use.
2 Includes both married and cohabiting couple family households.
3 A dependent child is a person in a household under 16 (whether or not in a family) or a person aged 16 to 18 who is a full-time student in a family with parent(s).

Source: Census 2001, Office for National Statistics; Census 2001, General Register Office for Scotland

among the highest within the European Union,[12] and the ONS/ DfT highlight that while the cost of motoring has remained relatively stable over the past 15 to 20 years when adjusted for inflation, the cost of bus and rail fares have risen by over 30 per cent since 1980.

Public transport also may not meet the transport needs for all due to poor frequency, reliability and network coverage in some areas, particularly in more rural locations. In Great Britain, a lack of adequate public transport was the most common transport problem cited by almost half of people who experienced transport problems in the 2001 NS Omnibus

Figure **5.14**

Trips made: by mode of transport for people in households with and without access to a car, 2002

Great Britain
Percentages

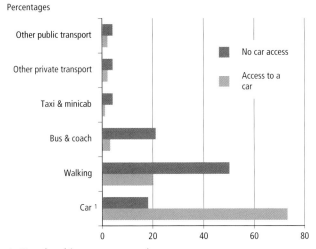

1 *Travel as driver or passenger in car.*

Source: National Travel Survey, Department for Transport

Survey. Fear of crime can also deter people from walking or waiting for, and travelling on, public transport. The NS Omnibus Survey found that 13 per cent of adults considered personal safety at bus stops to be poor, and 17 per cent were concerned over safety at rail or underground stations.

People with physical disabilities or health problems can have major problems in using both public and private transport. The NTS in 2002 found that 16 per cent of adults in Great Britain had a physical disability or long-standing health problem that made it difficult for them to go out on foot or use public transport. Mobility difficulties were particularly common with increasing age, steadily rising from five per cent of those aged 16 to 49 to 72 per cent of those aged 85 or over (1992 to 2000). Those with mobility difficulties can face problems with access to stations that require using stairs or escalators, and also in boarding buses and trains. Such obstacles can also be a problem for people with prams and pushchairs. In London, of the 275 Underground stations, only 40 do not require the use of steps or escalators. For disabled people, the cost of modifying or adapting a car to meet the needs of a physical disability can be a significant barrier to driving and car ownership. The DfT estimate that adding a wheelchair lift to a car costs around £6,000. Research by the DiPTAC in 2001/02, found that 60 per cent of households containing a disabled person in England and Wales had no access to a car, compared with 27 per cent of the general public.

Access to services

Transport problems can severely impact upon participation in the labour market and education. The 2000 GHS found that 53

per cent of workless households in Great Britain had no access to a car compared with 13 per cent of working households.[6] A lack of private or adequate public transport can limit where people seek employment, prevent people from attending interviews and lead to people turning down work. Research suggests that many job seekers consider transport a barrier to getting a job. According to the NS Omnibus Survey in 2001, 13 per cent of adults in Great Britain had not applied for a particular job in the past 12 months, and five per cent had turned down work because of transport problems.

Transport difficulties can limit the choice that parents make for their children, restrict participation in after-school clubs and activities, and can also be a barrier for involvement in post-compulsory education. Research shows that many students find transport costs hard to meet. The NS Omnibus Survey found that six per cent of young people aged 16 to 24 in Great Britain rejected training or further education in 2001 due to transport difficulties.

For many people, lack of access to a car causes difficulties in accessing services such as shops and health services (Table 5.15). In 2000/01, 38 per cent of people in Great Britain in households without access to a car stated that they had difficulties in accessing either their local chemist, General Practitioner (GP), local hospital, post office or main food shop, compared with 21 per cent with a car. Supermarkets, with a wide range of cheap food, are often located out of town and people without access to a car have the choice of making complex and long journeys by public transport or using more expensive local shops.

Poor access to health services means that some people do not seek medical help or miss appointments. According to the

Table **5.15**

Difficulty[1] in getting to services: by household car ownership, 2000/01

Great Britain   Percentages

	Household with access to a car	Households without access to a car
General Practitioner (GP)	4	11
Post Office	2	5
Main food shopping	5	13
Local hospital	17	31
Chemist	2	6
At least one service	21	38

1 *Finding services fairly or very difficult to access.*

Source: NS Omnibus Survey, Office for National Statistics

2001 NS Omnibus Survey, three per cent of people in Great Britain, missed, turned down or did not seek medical help because of transport problems experienced in the previous year. People without cars were also twice as likely to consider transport a barrier to participation in a range of social and leisure activities, including seeing friends and accessing leisure facilities.[13] The Commission for Integrated Transport in 2002 found that 29 per cent of people in England thought that better public transport would have a positive impact on their social lives.

Conclusion

In general, living standards are the visible product or outcome of other forms of inequality. In particular, variance in income is a strong predictor of people's access to material resources, socially perceived necessities and the type of neighbourhood in which they live. Basic resources such as shelter are necessary for life, while other resources such as socially perceived necessities or access to common goods and services have an impact upon quality of life, and the absence of such resources can contribute to people's feeling of isolation or exclusion from society. The quality of the local environment, including the physical environment, incidence of anti-social behaviour and crime, also contributes to people's quality of life, well-being and happiness. Access to reliable private or public transport is another indicator of living standards. A lack of transport, particularly for those in more rural areas, can create and reinforce inequalities in terms of people's access to heath care and opportunities for employment or education. While the cause and severity of issues differ, significant proportions of people are affected by a lack of material resources, decent housing, homelessness, transport and environmental problems.

References

1. Gordon D, Levitas R, Middleton S, Townsend P and Bradshaw J (2000) Poverty and Social Exclusion: Survey of Britain, York: Joseph Rowntree Foundation

2. Joseph Rowntree Foundation (2001) The impact of housing conditions on excess winter deaths, Ref N11, *http://www.jrf.org.uk/knowledge/findings/housing/n11.asp*

3. Department of Trade and Industry, Department for the Environment, Food, and Rural Affairs (2003), Detailed breakdowns of fuel poverty in England in 2001, version 2, July 2003, A summary report presenting data produced by the Building Research Establishment on behalf of the DTI and DEFRA.

4. Department for the Environment, Food, and Rural Affairs (2003) Warmer homes for millions, News Release March 2003 (81/03), *http://www.defra.gov.uk/news/2003/030304b.htm*

5. Department for Education and Skills (2002) Young People & Information and Communications Technology 2002 *http://www.becta.org.uk/page_documents/research/ngflseries_youngpeopleict.pdf*

6. Sykes W and Walker A (2002) Disadvantaged Households: Results from the 2000 General Household Survey Supplement A, Office for National Statistics *http://www.statistics.gov.uk/downloads/theme_social/GHSCrossTops.pdf*

7. Burrows R (2003) Poverty and home ownership in contemporary Britain, The Policy Press in association with the Joseph Rowntree Foundation, Ref 113, *http://www.jrf.org.uk/knowledge/findings/housing/113.asp*

8. Social Exclusion Unit (1998) Rough Sleeping – Report by the Social Exclusion Unit, *http://www.socialexclusion.gov.uk*

9. Griffiths S (2002) Addressing the health needs of rough sleepers, a paper to the Homelessness Directorate, Office of the Deputy Prime Minister, *http://www.odpm.gov.uk/stellent/groups/odpm_homelessness/documents/page/odpm_home_601532.pdf*

10. Coulthard M, Walker A, and Morgan A (2002) People's perceptions of their neighbourhood and community involvement, Results from the social capital module of the General Household Survey 2000, Office for National Statistics, *http://www.statistics.gov.uk/downloads/theme_social/Peoples_perceptions_social_capital.pdf*

11. Simmons J and Dodd T (eds) (2003) Crime in England and Wales 2002/03, Home Office Report 07/03, *http://www.homeoffice.gov.uk/rds/pdfs2/hosb703.pdf*

12. Commission for Integrated Transport (2001) European Best Practice in Delivering Integrated Transport (cited in Social Exclusion Unit (2003) Making the Connections: Final Report on Transport and social Exclusion, p31)

13. Ruston D (2002) Difficulty in Accessing Key Services, Office for National Statistics *http://www.statistics.gov.uk/downloads/theme_social/access_key_services/access_to_services.pdf*

Further reading

Office of the Deputy Prime Minister (2003) English House Condition Survey 2001, *http://www.odpm.gov.uk/stellent/groups/odpm_housing/documents/page/odpm_house_022942.pdf*

Health

Melissa Coulthard, Yuan Huang Chow,
Nirupa Dattani, Chris White, Allan Baker
and Brian Johnson

Chapter 6

Introduction

The health of the population has been improving steadily over the last century. However despite this general improvement, the gap in the main causes of death between those in the advantaged and disadvantaged groups widened in the latter part of the 20th century. Those in disadvantaged groups are more likely to die earlier and to be in poorer health compared with the rest of the population.

The reasons for these health inequalities are complex. There are links with people's social and demographic circumstances such as their educational attainment, occupation, income, type of housing, sex, ethnicity and where they live. These factors also relate to lifestyle behaviours such as smoking, drinking, diet and risk taking.

The Government has stated a commitment to tackling health inequalities and has set a national target for England to reduce inequalities in health outcomes by 10 per cent as measured by infant mortality and life expectancy at birth by the year 2010. The aim of this target is to narrow the health gap in childhood and throughout life between socio-economic groups and between the most disadvantaged areas and the rest of the country.[1]

Topics included in this review start with the early years and then focus on lifestyles, use of primary health services, health status and mental well being, and finally social differences in mortality.

Early years

A person's health and life chances can be influenced by social circumstances even before they are born. Smoking during pregnancy has implications for the baby's health, and low birthweight is a strong predictor of mortality in infancy and of lifelong poor health. Differences in infant mortality between routine and manual groups and the population as a whole provide one of the Government targets on health inequalities.

Smoking during pregnancy

Smoking during pregnancy affects the life chances of the unborn child. Pregnant women who smoke are more likely to miscarry, or to have pre-term deliveries and low birthweight babies. Their babies are more likely to die of sudden infant death, or to suffer from respiratory problems such as chest infections and asthma.[2]

Exposure to a parent's cigarette smoke during childhood can also have implications for long-term health due to the risks associated with passive smoking. In *Smoking Kills - A White Paper on Tobacco* the Government set a target in England to reduce the proportion of women who continue to smoke

during pregnancy to 18 per cent by the year 2005, and 15 per cent by 2010.[2]

The Infant Feeding Survey carried out in the United Kingdom in 2000 asked recent mothers about their smoking habits before, during and after pregnancy.[3] A fifth (20 per cent) smoked throughout their pregnancy, although most did cut down.

There is a strong relationship between smoking and socio-economic status (see Appendix, Part 2: Socio-economic classification) and this association was also seen among pregnant women (Figure 6.1). Only eight per cent of women in managerial and professional occupations smoked throughout pregnancy compared with 29 per cent of women in routine and manual occupations and 36 per cent of women who had never worked.

Figure **6.1**

Prevalence of smoking throughout pregnancy: by mother's NS-SEC, 2000

United Kingdom

Percentages

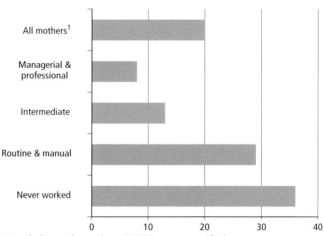

1 Includes mothers where NS-SEC was unclassified.

Source: Infant Feeding 2000 for Department of Health, Scottish Executive, National Assembly for Wales and Department of Health, Social Services and Public Safety in Northern Ireland

Smoking while pregnant is an example of the cycle of health inequalities. The socio-economic status of a child's parents has effects throughout life, starting even before birth. Children of smokers are much more likely to take up smoking themselves,[2] therefore continuing the health inequalities cycle. A life-course approach to health inequalities argues that health in later life is affected by a complex combination of circumstances that take place over time, including circumstances that happen before birth, such as parental smoking.[4]

Low birthweight

Birthweight is a commonly used indicator of the health status of babies. It is also a predictive indicator of health inequalities in later life. In England and Wales in 2002, the distribution of low birthweight (under 2500g) babies among singleton live births varied by mother's age and father's socio-economic status (Figure 6.2). For births that were solely registered by the mother no information about the father was recorded; therefore his occupation and consequently NS-SEC category are not known. Information about the father is collected only for births that either occur inside marriage or outside marriage where the birth is jointly registered by both parents.

Figure **6.2**

Low birthweight[1]: by mother's age, sole registration and father's NS-SEC, 2002

England & Wales

Percentages

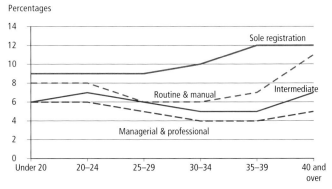

1 *Low birthweight among singleton live births. Where a singleton birth is a maternity leading to a single birth.*

Source: Birth registrations, Office for National Statistics

Overall, the incidence of low birthweight babies was highest (nine per cent) among sole registrations. This was followed by babies who were registered by both parents (within and outside marriage) whose fathers were in routine and manual occupations (seven per cent). It was lowest (five per cent) for babies with fathers in managerial and professional occupations. This pattern was apparent for mothers in each age group (Figure 6.2). However the magnitude of the difference between social groups and between sole and couple registrations varied by age of mother. The differences were smaller for mothers aged under 25 than for older mothers. Babies born to mothers aged 40 and over that were sole registrations were twice as likely to be of low birthweight compared with those born with fathers in the managerial and professional occupations.

The variation in the pattern of low birthweight should be viewed in the context of the overall distribution of births by mother's age (Figure 6.3). Women whose husbands/partners were in the managerial and professional group were more likely to have their babies at older ages whereas single mothers (sole registration) were more likely to have babies at younger ages. In particular, where the father was in the managerial and

professional group only two per cent of mothers were aged under 20 and 40 per cent were aged 30 to 34. Among babies that were registered solely by the mother, these proportions were 26 per cent and 14 per cent respectively. It can therefore be seen that in each social group, the incidence of low birthweight tends to be lowest at or around the ages at which it is common to have babies.

Figure **6.3**

Singleton[1] live births: by mother's age, sole registration and father's NS-SEC, 2002

England & Wales

Percentages

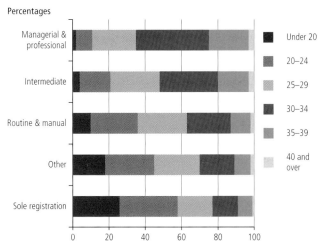

1 *A singleton baby is one that results from a maternity leading to a single birth.*

Source: Birth registrations, Office for National Statistics

Infant mortality

The infant mortality rate (deaths at ages under one year per 1,000 live births) has long been regarded as an important indicator of the health of a population. Over the twentieth century, infant mortality rates dropped significantly in response to improved living conditions, diet and sanitation, advances in medical science and the availability of healthcare. But despite such overall improvements, important differentials exist by father's socio-economic status, birthweight, type of birth registration and mother's country of birth.

Infant mortality rates have consistently shown large differences by socio-economic status. During the period 1994 to 2002, the highest infant mortality rate was for babies registered by the mother alone (sole registration). For babies registered by both parents, the infant mortality rate was highest for babies with fathers in semi-routine and routine occupations compared with all other groups (Figure 6.4 - see overleaf). Conversely, babies with fathers in managerial and professional occupations had the lowest infant mortality rate. But the magnitude of the difference in infant mortality rates by NS-SEC and between sole and couple registrations varied during this period.

Figure **6.4**

Infant mortality rate: by sole registration and father's NS-SEC[1], 2002

England & Wales

Rate per 1,000 live births

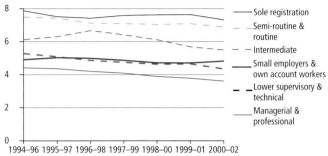

1 NS-SEC has been approximated on infant deaths prior to 2001. See Appendix, Part 6: Infant mortality by socio-economic status.

Source: Office for National Statistics

Between 1994 and 2002, the overall infant mortality rate decreased by 16 per cent from 6.2 per 1,000 live births to 5.2. The infant mortality rate of babies with fathers in the semi-routine and routine group decreased by five per cent from 7.3 to 6.9 per 1,000.

Lifestyles

Health-related behaviours have a major impact on health. This section looks at how cigarette smoking, alcohol consumption and obesity (which reflects factors such as diet and exercise) vary with sex, socio-economic group and ethnicity.

Smoking

The proportion of people who smoke tobacco has decreased considerably for both men and women aged 16 and over in the United Kingdom.[5,6] Data for Great Britain shows that levels of smoking have decreased since they were first recorded in the General Household Survey (GHS) in 1974. The prevalence of cigarette smoking fell substantially in the 1970s and the early 1980s (from 45 per cent in 1974 to 35 per cent in 1982). From 1982 the rate of decline slowed and since the early 1990s it has been almost stable, when the percentage of people smoking remained at 27 to 28 per cent until 2002.[5] Data on Northern Ireland, collected by the Continuous Household Survey (CHS) since 1983, show a similar pattern of decline.[6] In 2002 about a quarter (26 per cent) of adults were current smokers in the United Kingdom.[5,6]

The reduction in levels of smoking has been more dramatic for men than women.[5,6] For example, the proportion of men in Great Britain who have never smoked substantially increased from 25 per cent in 1974 to 46 per cent in 2002. For women

the rise was less dramatic, from 49 per cent to 54 per cent over the same time period.[5]

During the 1990s there was a decrease in the number of heavy cigarette smokers (those smoking twenty or more a day) and a reduction in the average tar levels in each cigarette smoked in Great Britain.[5] However smoking remains a major cause of ill health and death. It is the largest single cause of preventable deaths in the United Kingdom and is the main avoidable risk factor for coronary heart disease and cancer.[2]

In the United Kingdom the proportion of smokers has reduced in both manual and non-manual Registrar General's socio-economic groups (see Appendix, Part 2: Socio-economic classification). However, those in manual groups have been consistently more likely to smoke than those in non-manual groups. For men in Great Britain, the difference between the groups has remained at about 15 percentage points since 1976. For women, the difference increased between 1974 and 1998 from seven to ten percentage points. However, as the number of people who smoke decreased the relative difference between manual and non-manual smokers has increased. For example in 1974 men in Great Britain from manual backgrounds were 24 per cent more likely to smoke than men in non-manual groups. In 2000 they were 52 per cent more likely to smoke. The equivalent figures for women were 18 per cent and 36 per cent.[7] Overall the pattern is similar in Northern Ireland; smoking prevalence has been falling for both groups, but levels remain greater among the manual group. The likelihood of a man smoking has been around twice as great for the manual occupations compared with non-manual for much of the period since the mid-1980s.[8]

Smoking is currently the main cause of higher death rates in the manual as compared with the non-manual group.[9] Consequently the Government has set targets for England, not only to reduce the prevalence of cigarette smoking among adults,[2] but also to reduce the proportion of smokers in households headed by someone in a manual group from 32 per cent in 1998 to 26 per cent by 2010.[10] In 2002 the prevalence of cigarette smoking in England in this group was 31 per cent. This figure is based on weighted data, where the 1998 baseline figure is based on unweighted data. Weighting was introduced to the survey in 2000 and increased reported prevalence by about one percentage point.

Data for Great Britain for 2002 have also been analysed by NS-SEC (Figure 6.5). The pattern is broadly similar to that found using socio-economic group. About a third (32 per cent) of adults living in a household where the reference person was in a routine or manual occupation were current smokers compared with less than a fifth (19 per cent) of those in managerial and professional households. In addition, adults in routine or manual households were twice as likely as those in managerial and professional households to smoke their first cigarette (a measure of nicotine dependence) within five minutes of waking: 18 per cent compared with nine per cent. Adults in routine or manual households were also more likely to say that they would find it difficult to stop smoking (50 per cent) than people in managerial and professional households.[5]

Figure **6.5**

Prevalence of cigarette smoking: by sex and NS-SEC[1], 2002

Great Britain

Percentages

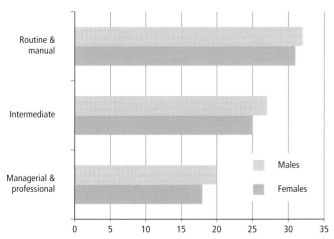

1 For persons aged 16 and over, and based on the current or last job of the household reference person. See Appendix, Part 6: Household reference person.

Source: General Household Survey, Office for National Statistics

Bangladeshi men were the most likely group in England to smoke cigarettes (44 per cent in 1999), followed by White Irish (39 per cent) and Black Caribbean men (35 per cent) (Figure 6.6). Men from each of these ethnic groups were more likely to smoke than men in the general population (27 per cent). Chinese men (17 per cent) were the least likely to smoke.[11] Similar proportions of Pakistani (26 per cent) and Indian (23 per cent) men smoked as in the general population.

Like men, White Irish and Black Caribbean women had the highest smoking rates in 1999 (33 per cent and 25 per cent respectively), although only White Irish women had a rate higher than the general population (27 per cent). However, unlike men, women in every other minority ethnic group were much less likely to smoke than women in the general population. Patterns of cigarette smoking among the minority ethnic groups remained the same after allowing for differences in their age structures.

Figure **6.6**

Current cigarette smoking: by ethnic group and sex, 1999

England

Percentages

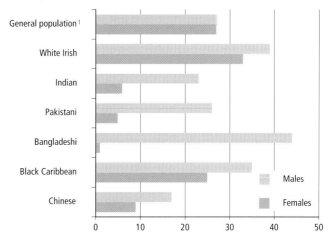

1 For a definition of general population see Appendix, Part 6: Health Survey for England.

Source: Health Survey for England, Department of Health

Although very few Bangladeshi women smoked cigarettes, a relatively large proportion (26 per cent) chewed tobacco. This method of using tobacco was also popular among Bangladeshi men (19 per cent), but they tended to use it in conjunction with cigarettes.

In the general population, men and women were equally likely to be smokers. However, among minority ethnic groups women were less likely to smoke than men. The sex difference was particularly marked among the Bangladeshi group.

Smoking behaviour is strongly related to a person's socio-economic class. People from lower socio-economic classes are more likely to smoke than those from higher classes.

Part of the pattern of smoking among the minority ethnic groups is explained by the socio-economic differences among the groups. For example, Bangladeshi men were over represented in the lowest socio-economic class (semi-routine or routine occupations), and these men also had the highest rates of smoking.

Drinking

Excessive alcohol consumption can cause disease, and ultimately death, mainly through liver diseases, such as cirrhosis, as well as other conditions such as cancer, heart disease and strokes. Fatal or debilitating injury can also result from drunken behaviour.

It is acknowledged that 'binge drinking' is more damaging to health than drinking moderately over several days or a week. Therefore the Government has set benchmarks of the recommended safe maximum amount to drink in a day: four units of alcohol for men, and three units for women.[12]

Smoking is more prevalent among those in routine and manual households than those in managerial and professional households. However, excessive drinking does not follow this pattern. Data for Great Britain for 2002 show that adults from households where the reference person is in a managerial and professional occupation were slightly more likely to have exceeded the Government benchmarks for safe drinking (32 per cent), compared with people in routine and manual households (29 per cent). There are small differences between the socio-economic groups for both men and women (Figure 6.7).[5] Data for Northern Ireland show a similar pattern among men: in 2001 men in non-manual occupations were more likely than men in manual occupations to drink more than the recommended sensible weekly level of alcohol, which for men is defined as 21 units. However, women from manual groups were more likely to drink at levels in excess of the recommended 14 units of alcohol than their non-manual counterparts.[13]

Figure **6.7**

People exceeding Government benchmarks for safe drinking[1] in last week: by NS-SEC[2] and sex, 2002

Great Britain

Percentages

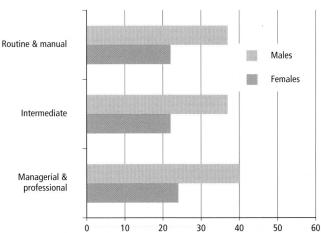

1 Drank more than 4 units (men) or 3 units (women) on at least one day last week.
2 For persons aged 16 and over, and based on the current or last job of the household reference person.

Source: General Household Survey, Office for National Statistics

A health survey was carried out in England in 1999 that concentrated on the health of minority ethnic groups.[11] The Irish were the group with the highest proportion exceeding the

Government guidelines on alcohol consumption. For example 58 per cent of White Irish men exceeded the benchmarks compared with 46 per cent of the male general population (see Appendix, Part 6: Health Survey for England). All other minority ethnic groups were less likely to exceed the Government guidelines and were more likely to be non-drinkers, or to drink smaller quantities less frequently compared with the general population. This was particularly true for Pakistani and Bangladeshi groups, the majority of whom are Muslim, a religion which prohibits drinking (Figure 6.8).

Figure **6.8**

Adults drinking above recommended daily alcohol guidelines[1]: by ethnic group and sex, 1999

England

Percentages

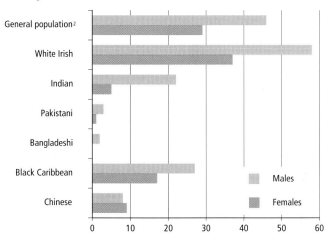

1 Government guidelines are no more than 3–4 units per day for men and 2–3 units per day for women.
2 For a definition of general population see Appendix, Part 6: Health Survey for England.

Source: Health Survey for England, Department of Health

Obesity

Diets rich in fat and excess sugars, combined with non-active lifestyles, have resulted in a greater prevalence of obesity in nearly all developed countries. Obesity has major health implications, including increased risk of diseases such as coronary heart disease, cancer and diabetes.[14] It is estimated that obesity causes more than 9,000 premature deaths each year in England and reduces life expectancy on average by nine years.[15]

The Health Survey for England (HSE) shows a pattern of increasing obesity prevalence in both adults and children. The increase in the proportion of children who are overweight or obese is of particular concern. Between 1995 and 2002 obesity rates for boys aged two to 15 in England almost doubled, increasing from three per cent to nearly six per cent. For girls of the same age, the rate rose from five per cent to eight per cent.[16]

Although the prevalence of obesity in children increased over time among both the manual and non-manual classes, the rise was more pronounced among manual classes across all sex and age groups.[16] For girls, obesity prevalence was lowest in households where the reference person was in a managerial or professional occupation (five per cent) and highest where the reference person was in an intermediate or semi-routine or routine occupation (eight per cent and nine per cent, respectively) (Figure 6.9). For boys there was no statistically significant variation.

Figure **6.9**

Age-standardised[1] obesity[2] prevalence estimates among children aged 2 to 15: by NS-SEC[3] and sex, 2001-02

England

Percentages

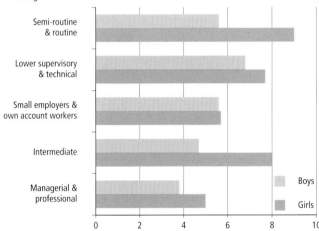

1 See Appendix, Part 6: Age-standardisation.
2 Obesity is classified using body mass index (BMI), which is calculated as weight (kg) divided by height squared (m²). In this chart, obesity is defined as those who would have been in the top five per cent of boys or girls based on UK BMI measurement.
3 NS-SEC of household reference person.

Source: Health Survey for England, Department of Health

More than a fifth of males and females aged 16 and over in England were classified as obese in 2002. Obesity among adults is related to social class, with the association being stronger for women than men. For example, in 2002, 35 per cent of women in routine occupations were classified as obese compared with 16 per cent in higher managerial and professional occupations.[17]

Data from the 1999 HSE found differences in the prevalence of adult obesity between minority ethnic groups. Bangladeshi and Chinese men had low prevalence of obesity, at five per cent and six per cent respectively, compared with men in the general population (19 per cent). Among women the differences in rates between minority ethnic groups were much greater than for the men. Prevalence of obesity among Black Caribbean and Pakistani women was higher than among

women in the general population: 32 per cent and 26 per cent respectively, compared with 21 per cent.[11] These observed findings were confirmed after adjusting obesity prevalence for age.

After age standardisation (see Appendix, Part 6) no significant differences in the prevalence of obesity were seen between men of non-manual and manual social classes of the same minority ethnic group. For women, the age-standardised prevalence of obesity was higher in manual than in non-manual social classes in most minority ethnic groups, although the differences were only significant for Bangladeshi women.[11]

Use of primary health care services

General Practitioner (GP) surgeries and health centres provide diagnosis of illness alongside access to a variety of services including smoking cessation, healthy eating advice, immunisation programmes, treatment and counselling. GPs provide front-line public health interventions. Therefore it is important that these are available to everyone within the local community.

Results from the GHS in 2002/03 for Great Britain show that females are more likely than males to consult their GP. Children under five years old and the elderly (those aged 75 or over) were most likely to consult their GP, whereas young people aged five to 15 years old were least likely to have GP consultations.[5] The equivalent survey in Northern Ireland for 2002/03 also found that females are more likely to consult their GP than males (20 per cent compared with 15 per cent), and that those aged over 65 are most likely to consult their GP compared with other age groups.[18]

Economically inactive men visited their GP on average seven times per year compared with three times for men who were working. Economically inactive and unemployed women were also more likely to visit their GP, with eight and seven visits per year respectively compared with five made by working women. However, people who are economically inactive may be unable to work owing to an illness and therefore would be expected to consult their GP more frequently.[5]

The lack of consultation with a GP is also an important health issue, as individuals may be missing out on preventative services. Data for England on GP consultation rates by ethnic group show that Pakistani women were more likely and Chinese women less likely to visit their GP compared with women in the general population; nine and five visits per year respectively (Figure 6.10 - see overleaf). Bangladeshi men were more likely to consult their GP than any other ethnic group, on average seven visits per year compared with four by males in the general population and three by Chinese men (who were the least likely to consult their GP).[11]

Figure **6.10**

NHS GP consultations[1]: by ethnic group and sex, 1999

England

Consultations per year

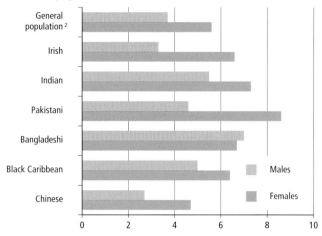

1 Annual contact rate per person.
2 For a definition of general population see Appendix, Part 6: Health
   Survey for England.

Source: Health Survey for England, Department of Health

Language barriers that inhibit individuals from using health services are another important inequality issue. The NHS survey of patients asked people whether or not there was anyone available to help with interpreting when visiting the GP or health centre. Forty three per cent relied on a relative or friend, 16 per cent on someone from the surgery or health centre and 41 per cent said there was no one available to interpret for them.[19]

In 1998, and four years later in 2002, a national survey of NHS patients was carried out in England looking at people's opinions of their GP service.[20,21] There were distinct differences by ethnic group. Minority ethnic respondents, particularly the Pakistani and Bangladeshi group, tended to take a less favourable view of their GP service than the White population. For example the Pakistani and Bangladeshi group was less likely to report getting an appointment on the day they wanted, felt the doctor did not answer their questions and were more likely to have been put off going to see the GP because of inconvenient surgery hours.

Overall, there were very few regional differences in GP services. The main difference was between London and other regions. For example, waiting times were longer in London: in 2002, 77 per cent had to wait two or more days for a GP appointment, compared with the overall figure for England of 67 per cent.[21]

Health status

This section looks at self-reported health and limiting long-term illness by socio-economic classifications and ethnicity.

Self-reported health

Although questions on self-reported general health have been used in both specialised health surveys and in general surveys of the population, 2001 was the first time that a general health question was included in the Census. The question asked people to rate their health over the last twelve months. The possible responses were "good", "fairly good" or "not good" and the question required a separate response for each person in the household.

Age-standardised reporting of poor health in the United Kingdom was lowest among professional and managerial occupations and highest in the long-term unemployed and never worked category (Figure 6.11). The second highest proportion of men reporting poor health was among those in semi-routine and routine occupations (nine per cent). This rate was just over twice that of men in professional and managerial groups (four per cent). The pattern was fairly similar for women. The highest rates among women were in the long-term unemployed and never worked category (20 per cent), followed by the lower supervisory (nine per cent) and the semi-routine and routine occupations (eight per cent). The lowest rates for women were in the professional and managerial groups (five per cent).

When most measures of health are analysed by the former Registrar General's Social Class groupings (see Appendix, Part 2: Socio-economic classification), a gradient is usually seen with increasingly poor health apparent in the lower social class

Figure **6.11**

Age-standardised poor health[1]: by NS-SEC[2] and sex, 2001

United Kingdom

Percentages

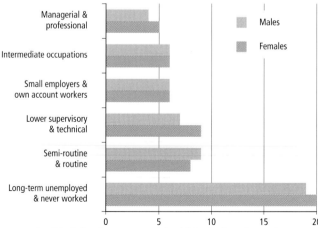

1 Poor health defined as 'not good' health in the last 12 months.
2 For persons aged 16–74.

Source: Census 2001, Office for National Statistics; Census 2001, General Register Office for Scotland; Census 2001, Northern Ireland Statistics and Research Agency

groups. Although NS-SEC is a different socio-economic classification, the marked difference in health between professional and managerial occupations at one extreme, and routine occupations at the other is still evident.

Census data have also been used to look at NS-SEC inequalities in self-reported health within and between the countries of Great Britain and the regions of England.[22] In each of the NS-SEC groups, Wales and North East and North West England had the highest rates of self-reported poor health. Scotland and London had the largest health divide by NS-SEC. In Scotland, routine workers were almost three times more likely to rate their health as poor compared with those in higher managerial or professional occupations (rate ratios of 2.9 for men and 2.8 for women). The equivalent figures in London were 2.9 for men and 2.4 for women. The lowest rate ratios for men were in the East (2.4) and were in the South West for women (1.8).

Ethnic variations in health represent an important dimension of health inequality in Britain. Pakistani and Bangladeshi men and women in England and Wales reported the highest rates of 'not good' health in 2001 (Figure 6.12). Pakistanis had age-standardised rates of 'not good' health of 13 per cent (men) and 17 per cent (women). The age-standardised rates for Bangladeshis were 14 per cent (men) and 15 per cent (women). These rates, which take account of the difference in age structures between the ethnic groups, were around twice that of their White British counterparts. Chinese men and women were the least likely to report their health as 'not good'. Women

were more likely than men to rate their health as 'not good' across most groups. Only in the White Irish group were men more likely than women to report their health as 'not good'.

Limiting long-term illness

Self-reported limiting long-term illness (LLTI) has been used frequently to profile inequalities in health by sex, socio-economic circumstances and ethnicity. LLTI is a generic term for a chronic condition that limits a person's activities or work they can do. It is important to measure the prevalence of limiting, chronic illness, because of the high cost in terms of quality of life of those affected, the reduced ability to participate in the labour market, and the likely need to use health and social care services.

Age-standardised LLTI prevalence by NS-SEC for both sexes produces a very similar pattern to self-reported health by NS-SEC (Figure 6.13). At the 2001 Census prevalence of LLTI in the United Kingdom was lowest in men and women in professional and managerial occupations (nine per cent and ten per cent, respectively) and highest among the long-term unemployed and those who have never worked (43 per cent among men and 36 per cent among women).[23] Excluding the long-term unemployed and those who have never worked, rates of LLTI were highest in the semi-routine and routine group among men (16 per cent) and highest in the semi-routine and routine group, and the lower supervisory and technical group among women (15 per cent).

Figure **6.12**

Age-standardised poor health[1]: by ethnic group and sex, 2001

England & Wales

Percentages

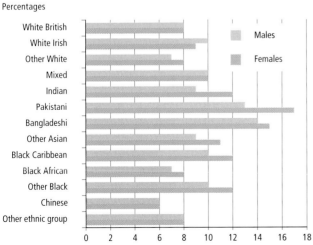

1 Poor health defined as 'not good' health in the last 12 months for persons aged 16–74.

Source: Census 2001, Office for National Statistics

Figure **6.13**

Age-standardised limiting long-term illness: by NS-SEC[1] and sex, 2001

United Kingdom

Percentages

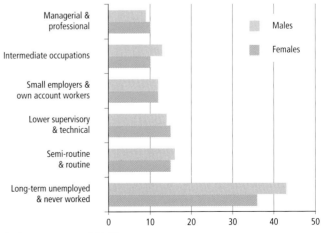

1 For persons aged 16–74.

Source: Census 2001, Office for National Statistics; Census 2001, General Register Office for Scotland; Census 2001, Northern Ireland Statistics and Research Agency

There were marked variations in rates of LLTI between different ethnic groups in England and Wales (Figure 6.14). After taking account of the different age structures of the groups, Pakistani and Bangladeshi men and women had the highest rates of LLTI. Rates were around one and a half times higher than the White British population. Chinese men and women had the lowest rates.

Figure **6.14**

Age-standardised limiting long-term illness: by ethnic group and sex, 2001[1]

England & Wales

Percentages

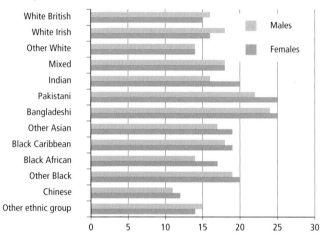

1   For persons aged 16–74.

Source: Census 2001, Office for National Statistics

In some groups the difference between men and women in their rates of LLTI was much greater than in others. In the Indian, Pakistani, Black Caribbean and Black African groups, women had higher rates than men. In the White British and White Irish groups men had higher rates than women.

Mental health

Mental illness was identified as one of the key areas for action in *The Health of the Nation*,[24] a White Paper published by the Department of Health in 1992 and subsequently in *Our Healthier Nation*[25] and *The NHS Plan*.[26] Frameworks for action have been set out in the *Health of the Nation Mental Illness Key Area Handbook*,[27] *The Spectrum of Care*[28] and most recently in the *National Service Framework for Mental Health*.[29]

People with common mental disorders, for example anxiety and depression, can suffer poorer social functioning and physical health[30] and higher rates of mortality.[31]

A survey of psychiatric morbidity among adults[32] assessed the prevalence of common mental disorders in the week prior to interview using the revised version of the Clinical Interview

Schedule (CIS-R).[33,34] The CIS-R covers 14 areas of neurotic symptoms, such as sleep problems, depression and compulsions. Adding up the scores on all the symptoms covered produces a total CIS-R score that reflects the overall severity of neurotic symptoms. Total scores range between zero and 57. A score of 12 or above indicates significant levels of neurotic symptoms.

In Great Britain in 2000, 15 per cent of people were assessed as having neurotic symptoms. Women were more likely than men to report neurotic symptoms (19 per cent compared with 12 per cent). Prevalence of neurotic disorders is associated with social class (Figure 6.15). People with unskilled occupations (Registrar General's Social Class V) were more than twice as likely to report neurotic disorders compared with those in professional occupations (Registrar General's Social Class I) (20 per cent compared with nine per cent).[32]

Figure **6.15**

Prevalence of neurotic disorders[1]: by social class, 2000[2]

Great Britain

Percentages

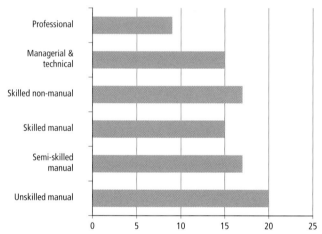

1   The prevalence of neurotic symptoms in the week prior to interview was assessed using the revised version of the Clinical Interview Schedule (CIS-R). A score of 12 or more indicates the presence of significant neurotic symptoms.
2   Adults aged 16–74.

Source: Survey of Psychiatric Morbidity among Adults in Great Britain, Office for National Statistics

In 2000 a survey was carried out in England that looked specifically at ethnic differences in mental health.[35] Once age structures were accounted for, the prevalence of neurotic disorders was similar across all ethnic groups. The only statistically significant difference was that Bangladeshi women had lower rates of neurotic disorders compared with White women.

Mortality

Social differences in death rates and life expectancy are stark reminders of the continuing impact of health inequalities. In 2001 the Government announced a national health inequality target to reduce inequalities in health outcome by 10 per cent as measured by infant mortality and life expectancy by 2010.[36]

Life expectancy by social class

The Independent Inquiry into Inequalities in Health, chaired by Sir Donald Acheson, highlighted the relative widening of the gap in life expectancy (see Appendix, Part 6) between advantaged and disadvantaged groups in society.[37]

Social class differences in life expectancy are often used to make comparisons of the health status of advantaged and disadvantaged groups in society and to track changes over time. Analysis of figures for England and Wales from 1972 to 1999 found sizeable inequalities in life expectancy in all periods analysed. Discrete time periods were chosen to ensure that a sufficient number of death events accrued in order to create more precise estimates of relative risk trends. Between 1972 and 1976, the male life expectancy at birth in professional occupations (Registrar General's Social Class I) was 72 years, compared with 66.5 years for men in unskilled manual occupations (Registrar General's Social Class V) (a gap of five and a half years). By the period 1997 to 1999, the gap in male life expectancy at birth between professional occupations and unskilled manual occupations had grown to 7.4 years. In women, the gap in life expectancy between professional occupations and unskilled manual occupations was 5.3 years between 1972 and 1976 and 5.7 years between 1997 and 1999[38] (Figure 6.16).

While substantial differences in social class life expectancy continued to be present during the 1970s, 1980s and 1990s, there was a narrowing in the male life expectancy divide during the 1990s both at birth and at age 65. This narrowing in life expectancy between professional occupations and unskilled manual occupations reflects the relative improvement in the mortality of men in unskilled occupations, compared with men in professional occupations. Differences in the trend in life expectancy at 65 were much less sizeable. This suggests that changes in life expectancy differences during the 1990s were driven by changes in mortality at younger ages.

Life expectancy by local authority

Life expectancy at birth was first used to illustrate diversity in the health status of populations in different parts of England and Wales in the 1840s. It has been used in recent years to identify geographic inequalities in health. Data for the years

Figure **6.16**

Life expectancy[1] at birth: by social class and sex, 1997-99

England & Wales

Years

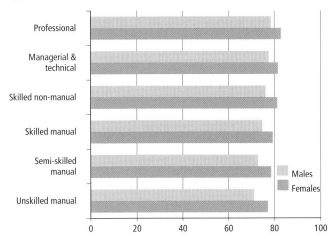

1 See Appendix, Part 6: Life expectancy.

Source: Longitudinal Study, Office for National Statistics

1999 to 2001 are illustrated in Figure 6.17a for males and Figure 6.17b females – (see overleaf). The results were produced by aggregating deaths and population data for the three-year period, to ensure that they were sufficiently robust. Local authorities have been ranked from highest to lowest and then divided into five equal groups (quintiles). The fifth of local authorities with the lowest life expectancy at birth (lightly shaded on the maps) are found most frequently in Scotland and the north of England, as well as in parts of south Wales, Northern Ireland and Greater London. Areas with the highest life expectancy (dark shading) are principally found in the south of England.

Within the United Kingdom in 1999 to 2001 Glasgow City was the local authority with the lowest life expectancy at birth for both males and females. Male life expectancy was only 68.7 years, over six and a half years less than for the United Kingdom (75.3 years) and over ten years less than for North Dorset, the local authority with the highest life expectancy at 79.3 years. For females there was a difference of just over seven years between the local authority with the highest life expectancy at birth, West Somerset (83.4 years), and Glasgow City (76.2 years). Manchester was the local authority with the lowest life expectancy at birth in England, and was the second lowest in the United Kingdom, for both males and females.

Social class inequalities in mortality

Much interest in recent years has focussed on social class gradients in mortality by cause of death, and how these gradients have changed over time. The trends described here are based on directly standardised rates for men and women aged 35 to 64 by social class between 1986 and 1999 in England and Wales.[39]

While mortality risk has fallen for all social classes since the mid-1980s, the rate of decline differs markedly depending on social class membership. Differential rates of decline impact fundamentally on the social class inequality divide, and can be used to measure the success of policies designed to tackle health inequalities.

Inequalities in overall male mortality between professionals, managers and technical workers and partly skilled and unskilled workers increased 3.6 per cent between 1986 and 1999 (Table 6.18 - see overleaf). This outcome was due to the slightly greater decline in mortality risk among men in professional, managerial and technical occupations (i.e. 25 per cent in social classes I&II) compared with men in partly skilled and unskilled

occupations (i.e. 22 per cent in social classes IV&V). Disease groups contributing most to this widening in inequality are ischaemic heart disease, cerebrovascular disease, respiratory diseases and lung cancer.

Over this 14 year period deaths from ischaemic heart disease (IHD) in men fell substantially in all social classes, but the pattern varied across time. Whereas falls were most sizeable between 1986–92 and 1993–96 in non-manual social classes, between 1993–96 and 1997–99 manual social classes experienced the largest falls. Consequently the social class gradient in IHD widened between 1986–92 and 1993–96, and then fell between 1993–96 and 1997–99. However taking the period as a whole, an increase in inequality was observed between professionals, managers and technical workers and partly skilled and unskilled workers.

Respiratory disease related deaths have a significant social profile in the periods examined, with partly skilled and unskilled

Figure **6.17a**

Life expectancy at birth: by local authority[1] and sex, 1999–2001

United Kingdom

Males

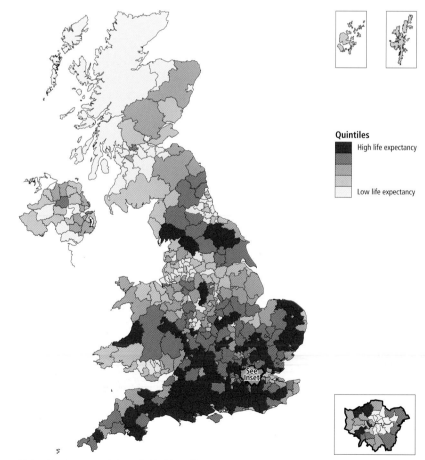

1   Local authorities ranked from highest to lowest and then divided into five groups.

Source: Office for National Statistics

workers five and a half times more likely to die in the period 1986–99 compared with professionals, managers and technical workers. Respiratory disease has the largest social class gradient for each period examined with no evidence of risk reducing as is the case with other major diseases such as IHD for which risk fell for social classes I&II, IIIM and IV&V.

Lung cancer deaths in males have been on the decline for over two decades, predominantly as a result of falls in the prevalence of smoking in earlier decades. Skilled manual workers was the only group to experience a significant reduction between 1986–92 and 1997–99, but remained at a significantly higher risk of lung cancer mortality than professional, managerial and technical workers for each period investigated.

Inequalities in overall mortality in women fell during this period (Table 6.18), although professional, managerial and technical

females workers remained at significantly lower risk of death compared with partly skilled and unskilled female workers for each period reported on. The rate of decline for partly skilled and unskilled female workers exceeded the fall for professional, managerial and technical workers in each comparison period causing the social gradient to contract by 8.4 per cent.

For women, gradients in the major causes of death were more irregular than in men, though there is no evidence of an inverse gradient existing. Between 1986–92 and 1997–99, IHD mortality in women showed falls of around 30 per cent in all social classes. Social class gradients persisted across time, but the difference between professionals, managers and technical workers, and partly skilled and unskilled workers failed to achieve significance in the period 1997–99. The IHD risk profile of manual workers declined more rapidly than that for non-manual workers between 1986–92 and 1997–99 with a non-significant difference observed in the period 1997–99.

Figure **6.17b**

Life expectancy at birth: by local authority[1] and sex, 1999–2001

United Kingdom

Females

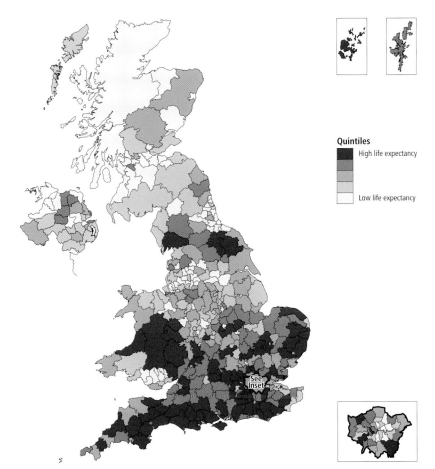

1 Local authorities ranked from highest to lowest and then divided into five groups.

Source: Office for National Statistics

© **Crown copyright . All rights reserved (ONS.GD272183.2004).**

Table **6.18**

All cause death rate[1]: by social class and sex

England & Wales		Rate per 100,000 people	
	1986–92	1993–96	1997–99
Males			
Professional, managerial & technical	460	379	347
Skilled non-manual	480	437	417
Skilled manual	617	538	512
Skilled, semi-skilled & unskilled manual	776	648	606
Non-manual	466	396	371
Manual	674	577	546
Females			
Professional, managerial & technical	274	262	237
Skilled non-manual	310	262	253
Skilled manual	350	324	327
Skilled, semi-skilled & unskilled manual	422	378	335
Non-manual	289	257	246
Manual	379	344	330

1 *Data have been directly age standardised using the European standard population. See Appendix, Part 6: Age-standardisation.*

Source: Longitudinal Study, Office for National Statistics

The social divide in cerebrovascular disease risk between professional, managerial and technical female workers and partly skilled and unskilled workers narrowed sharply between 1986–92 and 1997–99. Specifically, a significant 36 per cent gradient observed in the period 1986–92 had dissipated to a non-significant six per cent differential in the period 1997–99.

Women working in manual occupations were consistently at significantly higher risk of lung cancer mortality than women working in non-manual occupations for each period investigated. Despite a fall in lung cancer mortality in both groups, the manual group were more than twice as likely as the non-manual group to die from this disease in 1997–99.

Conclusion

The health of the population has improved steadily over the last century. However, the gap in health between those in the most disadvantaged groups and those in more advantaged groups in the main causes of death widened in the latter part of the 20th century. For example, between 1972 and 1976, the gap in life expectancy at birth for men between social classes I and V was five and a half years. By the period 1997 to 1999, the gap had grown to nearly seven and a half years.

The reasons for these health inequalities are complex. There are links with people's social, economic and demographic circumstances such as their educational attainment, occupation, income, type of housing, sex, ethnicity and where they live. For example, there is a strong relationship between NS-SEC and various health measures. People in routine and manual occupations were more likely than those in managerial and professional occupations to smoke during pregnancy, have babies with low birthweight, have babies that die in infancy, smoke, have poor self-reported health and suffer a limiting long-term illness.

References

1. Department of Health (2004) Technical Note for the Spending Review 2004 Public Service Agreement 2005–2008 - *http://www.dh.gov.uk/assetRoot/04/08/69/19/04086919.pdf*

2. Department of Health (1998) *Smoking Kills: A White Paper on tobacco. Saving lives: Our Healthier Nation*, London: The Stationery Office. *http://www.archive.official documents.co.uk/document/cm41/4177/4177.htm*

3. Hamlyn B, et al. (2002) Infant feeding 2000, London: The Stationery Office. *http://www.dh.gov.uk/PublicationsAndSta tistics/Publications/PublicationsStatistics/PublicationsStatistic sArticle/fs/en?CONTENT_ID=4079223&chk=UpJ4Sr*

4. Davey Smith G (ed) (2003) Health inequalities: lifecourse approaches. Bristol: Policy Press

5. Rickards L, et al. (2004) *Living in Britain. Results from the 2002 General Household Survey*, London: The Stationery Office. *www.statistics.gov.uk/downloads/theme_compendia/lib2002.pdf*

6. McWhirter L (2004) Equality and Inequalities in Health and Social Care in Northern Ireland: A Statistical Overview, Northern Ireland Statistics and Research Agency, Belfast. *http://www.dhsspsni.gov.uk/publications/2004/equality_inequalities/equality_inequalities.asp*

7. Walker A, et al. (2001) *Living in Britain. Results from the 2000 General Household Survey*, London: The Stationery Office, Table 8.8 and Drever F, et al. (2000) *Social Inequalities: 2000 edition*, London: The Stationery Office, Fig 2.28

8. Evandrou M and Falkingham J (2004) *Cigarette Smoking and Drinking Behaviour in Northern Ireland 1986–2000: A Cohort Analysis*. Department of Health, Social Services and Public Safety *http://www.dhsspsni.gov.uk/publications/2004/smoking_drinking_cohort_report.pdf*

9. Department of Health (2002) *Tackling health inequalities: Cross cutting review*, London: The Stationery Office

10. Department of Health (2000) *The NHS cancer plan*, London: The Stationery Office *http://www.dh.gov.uk/assetRoot/04/ 01/45/13/04014513.pdf*

11. Department of Health (2000) *Health of Minority Ethnic Groups. Health Survey for England 1999*. London: The Stationery Office *http://www.archive.official-documents.co.uk/document/doh/survey99/hse99.htm*

12. Department of Health (1995) *Sensible drinking: the report of an interdepartmental working group*, London: Department of Health

13. Miller R, Devine P and Schubotz D (2004) *Secondary Analysis of the 1997 and 2001 Northern Ireland Health and Social Wellbeing Surveys.* Department of Health, Social Services and Public Safety *http://www.dhsspsni.gov.uk/ publications/2004/ark04.pdf*

14. Donaldson L (2002) *Chief Medical Officer's Annual Report*, London: The Stationery Office

15. National Audit Office (2001) *Tackling obesity in England*, London: The Stationery Office

16. Department of Health (2003) *Health Survey for England 2002: The health of children and young people*, London: The Stationery Office *http://www.official-documents.co.uk/ document/deps/doh/survey02/hcyp/hcyp.htm*

17. Unpublished analysis from the Health Survey for England 2002, by the National Centre for Social Research, 2004

18. Table 6.2 - Continuous Household Survey Data table *http:// www.csu.nisra.gov.uk/surveys/survey.asp?id=1&details=3&t opicId=35*

19. Department of Health and Commission for Health Improvement. National Health Survey of Patients 2003 – *http://www.chi.nhs.uk/eng/surveys/index.shtml*

20. Airey C and Erens B (eds) (1999) *National survey of NHS patients*. General Practice 1998. London: Department of Health *http://www.dh.gov.uk/assetRoot/04/03/59/99/ 04035999.pdf*

21. Boreham R, et al. (eds) (2003) *National survey of NHS patients*. General Practice 2002. London: Department of Health *http://www.dh.gov.uk/assetRoot/04/02/40/50/ 04024050.pdf*

22. Doran T, et al. (2004) Is there a north-south divide in social class inequalities in health in Great Britain? Cross sectional study using data from the 2001 census. *BMJ* 328 (7447), pp 1043–45

23. Donkin A, Lee Y and Toson B. Implications of changes in the UK social and occupational classifications in 2001 for vital statistics. *Population Trends* 107 23–29. Spring 2002. London: The Stationery Office

24. Department of Health (1992) *White Paper. The health of the nation*, London: HMSO

25. Department of Health (1999) *White Paper. Saving lives: Our Healthier Nation,* London: The Stationery Office

26. Department of Health (2000) *The NHS Plan: A plan for investment. A plan for reform*, London: The Stationery Office

27. Department of Health (1994) *Health of the nation mental illness key area handbook*, London: HMSO

28. Department of Health (1996) *The spectrum of care*, London: The Stationery Office

29. Department of Health (1999) *National service framework for mental health*, London: The Stationery Office

30. Wells KB, Golding JM, Burnam MA (1998) Psychiatric disorder and limitations in physical functioning in a sample of the Los Angeles general population, *American Journal of Psychiatry* 145, 712–717. Cited in Nazroo J and Sproston K (eds) (2002) Ethnic minority psychiatric illness rates in the community (EMPIRIC). London: The Stationery Office (p25)

31. Murphy JM, Monson RR, Olivier DC, Sobol AM, Leighton AH (1987) Affective disorders and mortality, a general population study, *Archives of General Psychiatry* 44, 473– 480. Cited in Nazroo J and Sproston K (eds) (2002) Ethnic minority psychiatric illness rates in the community (EMPIRIC). London: The Stationery Office (p25)

32. Meltzer H, et al. (2002) *The social and economic circumstances of adults with mental disorders*, London: The Stationery Office

33. Lewis G and Pelosi A J (1990) *Manual of the revised clinical interview schedule (CIS-R)*, Institute of Psychiatry: London

34. Lewis G, Pelosi A J, Araya R C and Dunn G (1992) Measuring psychiatric disorder in the community: a standardised instrument for use by lay interviewers, Psychological Medicine, 22, 465–486

35. Nazroo J and Sproston K (eds) (2002) *Ethnic minority psychiatric illness rates in the community (EMPIRIC)*. London: The Stationery Office

36. Department of Health (2002) Improvement, expansion and reform: the next three years. Priorities and planning framework 2003–2006

37. Acheson D (1998) *Independent inquiry into inequalities in health,* London: The Stationery Office

38. Donkin A, Goldblatt P and Lynch K (2002) Inequalities in life expectancy by social class, 1972–99. *Health Statistics Quarterly* 15 5–15 London: The Stationery Office

39. White C, Van Galen F and Chow Y (2003) Trends in social class differences in mortality by cause, 1986–2000. *Health Statistics Quarterly* Winter pp 25–37. London: The Stationery Office.

Participation

Elizabeth Whiting

Chapter 7

Introduction

This publication has explored disadvantage in a number of areas of life: inequalities in education, the labour market, income and resources. Disadvantage experienced as a result of these inequalities can lead to barriers to involvement in social activities. Participation in clubs and organisations, contact with friends and family, engagement in civic activities - such as voting or attending a march, and volunteering are important in their own right and they have other associated social and economic benefits. Social participation provides networks of friends who can act as sources of social support and information, for example, when trying to find employment. However, certain groups of people, for a variety of reasons, can be denied access or do not have the opportunity to join in the activities of social groups, or are limited in the amount of social contact they have with others. People from disadvantaged backgrounds, such as those living in areas of high deprivation or those on low incomes, are less likely to participate in social activities than those from more advantaged backgrounds. The main barriers preventing participation include: lack of money and time, personal circumstances such as caring responsibilities, access to transport, fear of crime and lack of information.

Organisational membership

The United Kingdom has a long history of active civic and social networks with clubs and organisations set up for a variety of purposes ranging from recreational or social to political and environmental activities. For some people membership of these groups is passive, simply consisting of paying fees and receiving literature, but for others it is more active, involving social interaction or working with other members and can help to solve problems and initiate change. Participation in social organisations is important to people's quality of life and can have many positive social and economic outcomes such as improving health, reducing crime and building cohesive communities.[1] In 2001 the British Household Panel Survey (BHPS) asked adults aged 16 and over in Great Britain if they were a member of any social, political or community organisation. It also asked if they were actively involved in an organisation, defined as joining in the activities, of any of the organisations on a regular basis. The survey showed that there was considerable variation in the likelihood of joining or being active in an organisation between people with different socio-economic characteristics, such as age and life stage, qualifications, household composition and income.

Participation

According to the BHPS in 2001, 56 per cent of adults in Great Britain were members of at least one of a range of social,

political or community organisations and 46 per cent of adults were active in at least one organisation on a regular basis. Examples of such organisations include sports clubs, religious groups and parents associations.

Age has an impact on organisational membership. Young people and elderly people were least likely to be members or active in an organisation. Forty one per cent of people aged 16 to 24 were members of at least one organisation (Figure 7.1). Membership increased with age peaking at 64 per cent of people aged 45 to 54 and then declined gradually to 53 per cent for those aged 75–84, with a substantial drop to 41 per cent of people aged 85 and over.

Figure **7.1**

Membership of social organisations[1]: by age, 2001

Great Britain

Percentages

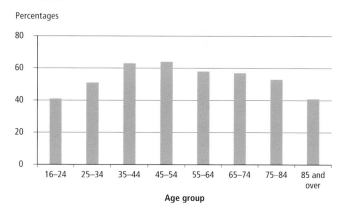

Age group

1   Social organisations include: political party, trade union, environmental group, parents association, tenants or residents group, religious group, voluntary service group, community group, social group, sports club, women's institute, women's group, professional organisation and pensioners' organisation.

Source: British Household Panel Survey, Institute for Social and Economic Research

A slightly different trend was evident in the proportion of people who were active in an organisation (Figure 7.2). Forty per cent of 16 to 24 year olds were active in an organisation. Levels of active participation, however, were broadly similar among people aged 35 to 84, with around half being active in at least one organisation. But as for membership, active participation was lowest for people aged 85 and over at 36 per cent.

It is clear that age influences participation, particularly membership of organisations. An age effect means that the likelihood of individuals participating in organisations changes at different stages in their life, determined by such demands as family commitments (marriage and children), work (when entered and left) and a reduction in energy and declining health status (as people get older). Results from British birth cohort studies suggest that changes in levels of organisational

Figure **7.2**

Active participation in social organisations[1]: by age, 2001

Great Britain

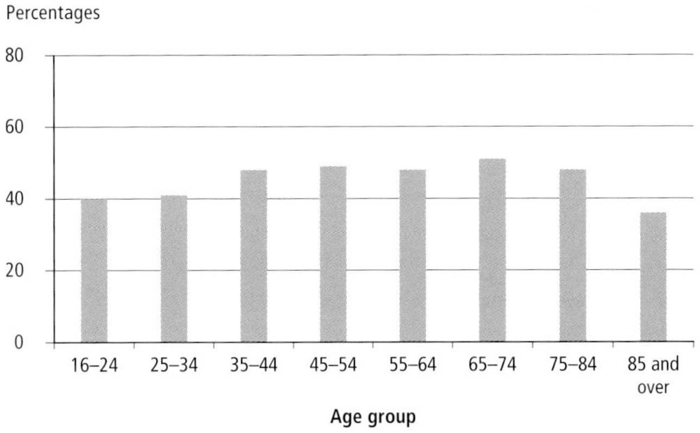

Percentages

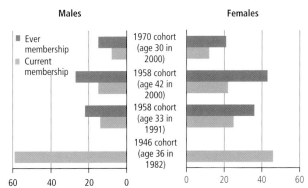

1   *Social organisations include: political party, trade union, environmental group, parents association, tenants or residents group, religious group, voluntary service group, community group, social group, sports club, women's institute, women's group, professional organisation and pensioners' organisation.*

Source: British Household Panel Survey, Institute for Social and Economic Research

Figure **7.3**

Social participation[1] in the 1946, 1958 and 1970 birth cohorts: by sex

Great Britain

Percentages

1   *Includes membership of a charity/voluntary group (environment), charity/voluntary group (other), women's groups, parents/school organisations, tenants/residents associations. Data for ever membership not available for 1946 cohort.*

Source: National Survey of Health and Development; 1958 National Child Development Study; 1970 British Cohort Study

membership are the result of cohort effects rather than age.[2] A cohort effect would suggest that there has been a change in society rather than in individuals and therefore different generations would be more or less likely to join or participate in social organisations.

The National Study of Health and Development, National Child Development Study and the British Cohort Study trace the lives of a sample of people born in one week in 1946, 1958 and 1970 respectively. Comparisons of participation rates of people in successive cohorts aged in their thirties showed that there was a marked decline in social participation (Figure 7.3). Fifty-nine per cent of men aged 36 in 1982 in the 1946 birth cohort were currently members of an organisation. For later birth cohorts this proportion was substantially lower at 14 per cent of men aged 33 in 1991 (from the 1958 birth cohort) and eight per cent of men aged 30 in 2000 (from the 1970 birth cohort). A similar trend was evident for women, although levels of membership appear greater than for men in the later cohorts. Where comparison was possible, the National Child Development Study showed that age effects were minimal. There was only a small increase in the percentage of people who said they were currently members or had ever been a member between ages 33 and 42 in the 1958 birth cohort. Twenty two per cent of men and 36 per cent of women aged 33 in 1991 said they had been members compared with 27 per cent of men and 43 per cent of women aged 42 in 2000.

There are other problems associated with the measurement of social and civic participation, particularly among young people.

Research suggests that standard quantitative measures of participation underestimate young people's involvement in social activities because they do not include the types of activities, that young people may be engaged in.[3] The social organisations included in the BHPS questionnaire, for example, are formal and include organisations such as parents associations, tenants groups, trade unions, professional and pensioners organisations, which are less likely to be relevant to the lives of young people. Until more appropriate questions are asked which measure the real extent of young people's participation, it is difficult to ascertain whether young people's apparent disengagement is the result of inaccurate measurement, or an age or cohort effect.

Household composition, which is related to age and life stage, also affects whether people were members or active in an organisation. In 2001 the BHPS showed that of all household types in Great Britain, couples with no children and non-related households were the most likely to be members of an organisation (60 per cent) and lone parents with dependent children were the least likely (36 per cent). In terms of active participation, lone parents with dependent children and lone parents with non-dependent children were also the least likely to be active in an organisation (Figure 7.4 - see overleaf). Thirty six per cent of lone parents with dependent children and 39 per cent of lone parents with non-dependent children actively participated in an organisation compared with the group with the highest percentage of participators - couples with no children - at 48 per cent.

Figure **7.4**

Active participation in social organisations[1]: by household type, 2001

Great Britain

Percentages

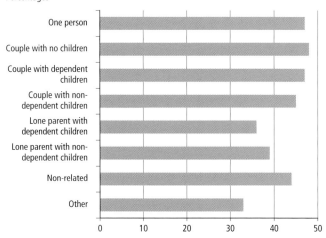

1   Social organisations include: political party, trade union, environmental group, parents association, tenants or residents group, religious group, voluntary service group, community group, social group, sports club, women's institute, women's group, professional organisation and pensioners' organisation.

Source: British Household Panel Survey, Institute for Social and Economic Research

Figure **7.5**

Active participation in social organisations[1]: by highest academic qualification, 2001

Great Britain

Percentages

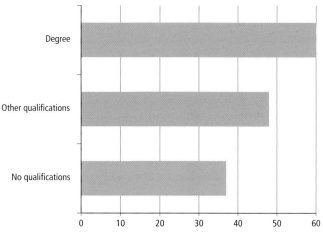

1   Social organisations include: political party, trade union, environmental group, parents association, tenants or residents group, religious group, voluntary service group, community group, social group, sports club, women's institute, women's group, professional organisation and pensioners' organisation.

Source: British Household Panel Survey, Institute for Social and Economic Research

People with higher educational qualifications are more likely to be employed and to be in higher paid occupations than people with lower or no qualifications (see Chapter 2: Education, training and skills). According to the BHPS, people with higher educational qualifications, those in employment and those earning higher incomes were all more likely to be a member of, or active in, a social organisation. Seventy seven per cent of people with a degree were members of an organisation, compared with 57 per cent of people with other qualifications and 45 per cent of people with no qualifications. People educated to degree level were also the most actively involved (Figure 7.5). Sixty per cent of those with a degree were active in at least one organisation, compared with 48 per cent and 37 per cent respectively for adults with other qualifications and no qualifications.

Employed people were the most likely to be a member of an organisation and unemployed people were the least likely, compared with the self-employed and economically inactive. Unemployed people were also the least likely to actively participate (Figure 7.6). Around half of the self-employed (50 per cent), employed (46 per cent) and economically inactive (46 per cent) were active in an organisation compared with a quarter of unemployed people (25 per cent).

Figure **7.6**

Active participation in social organisations[1]: by employment status, 2001

Great Britain

Percentages

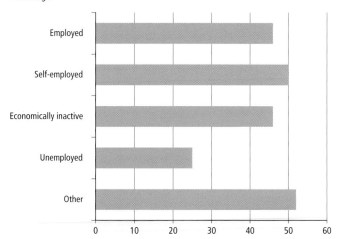

1   Social organisations include: political party, trade union, environmental group, parents association, tenants or residents group, religious group, voluntary service group, community group, social group, sports club, women's institute, women's group, professional organisation and pensioners' organisation.

Source: British Household Panel Survey, Institute for Social and Economic Research

Figure **7.7**

Active participation in social organisations[1]: by income quintiles, 1999

Great Britain

Percentages

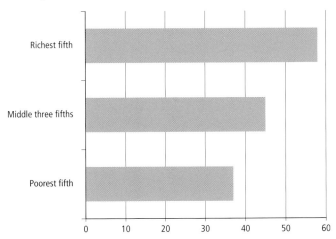

1 Social organisations include: political party, trade union, environmental group, parents association, tenants or residents group, religious group, voluntary service group, community group, social group, sports club, women's institute, women's group, professional organisation and pensioners' organisation.

Source: British Household Panel Survey, Institute for Social and Economic Research

People living in low income households were less likely to be active in organisations than those in higher income households (Figure 7.7). In 1999 in Great Britain 37 per cent of people in the poorest fifth of the income distribution actively participated, compared with 58 per cent of people in the richest fifth of the income distribution. Smaller financial resources are likely to contribute to the lower participation by groups such as the unemployed and lone parents.

Trends in organisational membership

There is a lack of reliable and accurate time series data showing levels of participation in social organisations and clubs, making it difficult to assess whether participation has increased or decreased over time. Thus one has to rely largely on an examination of membership figures, which are also limited, to distinguish time trends.

There has been a significant increase in membership in environmental organisations. Membership of the National Trust grew from 278,000 in 1971 to over three million in 2003, a growth of more than ten fold (Table 7.8). This is well above the five per cent population growth that has occurred in the United Kingdom since 1971. Several organisations have shown substantial rises since the late 1990s. Membership of the Woodland Trust more than doubled between 1997 and 2003, while membership of the Wildlife Trusts increased by 81 per cent. In contrast membership of the Civic Trust fell over the same period by 18 per cent.

Table **7.8**

Membership of selected environmental organisations

United Kingdom   Thousands

	1971	1981	1991	1997	2003
National Trust[1]	278	1,046	2,152	2,489	3,300
Royal Society for the Protection of Birds	98	441	852	1,007	1,037
Wildlife Trusts[2]	64	142	233	310	562
Civic Trust	214	..	222	330	272
The National Trust for Scotland	37	105	234	228	264
Greenpeace	..	30	312	215	226
Ramblers Association	22	37	87	123	141
Woodland Trust	..	..	63	60	127
Friends of the Earth	1	18	111	114	123
Campaign to Protect Rural England[3]	21	29	45	45	58
World Wide Fund for Nature[4]	12	60	227	241	320

1 Covers England, Wales and Northern Ireland.
2 Includes the Royal Society for Nature Conservation.
3 Previously called Council for the Protection of Rural England.
4 Data for 2003 unavailable. Data for 2002 used.

Source: Organisations concerned

Table 7.9

Population of Great Britain: by religion, April 2001

Great Britain

	Total population		Non-Christian religious population
	(Thousands)	(Percentages)	(Percentages)
Christian	41,015	71.82	..
Muslim	1,589	2.78	51.94
Hindu	558	0.98	18.25
Sikh	336	0.59	10.99
Jewish	267	0.47	8.74
Buddhist	149	0.26	4.88
Any other religion	159	0.28	5.20
No religion	8,596	15.05	..
Religion not stated	4,434	7.76	..
All non-Christian religious population[1]	3,059	5.36	100
All population	57,104	100	.

1 Excludes people who had no religion and those who did not state their religion.

Source: Census 2001, Office for National Statistics; Census 2001, General Register Office for Scotland

The 2001 Census was the first to include a question on religion (see Appendix, Part 7: Religion in the 2001 Census). Table 7.9 shows that Christianity is the main religion in Great Britain comprised of 72 per cent of the population. People with no religion formed the second largest group (15 per cent). About five per cent of the population belonged to a non-Christian religious denomination. Muslims formed the largest religious denomination after Christians (2.8 per cent), followed by Hindus (1.0 per cent) and then Sikhs (0.6 per cent).

A different Census question was asked in Northern Ireland compared with Great Britain. The community background of the respondent was identified; this referred to those belonging to or brought up in a particular religion (see Appendix, Part 7: Religion in the 2001 Census). People from a Protestant community made up the largest group in Northern Ireland in 2001 (53 per cent), followed by people from a Catholic community background (44 per cent).

Despite high levels of respondents identifying with a religion, actual attendance at religious meetings is much lower. The British Social Attitudes Survey (BSA) asked 'Do you regard yourself as belonging to any particular religion? If so which?' and 'Apart from such special occasions as weddings, funerals and baptisms, how often nowadays do you attend meetings or

services connected with your religion?' Eighteen per cent of people with a religious affiliation attended a place of worship at least once a week in 2002, only one per cent less than in 1983. However, nearly half of the people who professed a religion attended a place of worship less than once a year.[4] This survey showed that the proportion of people who professed no religion at all grew from 31 per cent in 1983 to 40 per cent in 2002. The observed differences in the extent of religious affiliation are likely to be the result of the different questions asked.

People who attended a place of worship or who were members or active in a religious group were more likely to be older and have higher academic qualifications. The BHPS showed that in 2001, 24 per cent of people aged between 75 and 84 attended a religious service once a week compared with five per cent of 16 to 24 year olds. Nineteen per cent of people with higher academic qualifications were members of a religious group compared with nine per cent of people with other qualifications and 11 per cent of people with no qualifications.

Another type of organisation that has experienced a substantial decline in membership is trade unions. The Department of Trade and Industry found that trade union membership dropped from a peak in 1979 of 13.2 million to 7.8 million in 2001. The BHPS showed that of those employed, the age group most likely to be members of a trade union were those aged between 35 and 44 (27 per cent). Young people aged 16 to 24 were the least likely to be members of a trade union (11 per cent). People employed in managerial and professional occupations and semi-routine and routine occupations were also more likely to be members of a trade union than those from other socio-economic groups: 37 per cent of those in managerial and professional occupations and 27 per cent in the semi-routine and routine occupations, compared with between 10 and 15 per cent of people in other socio-economic groups.

Women's organisations have also experienced a decline in membership (Table 7.10). According to figures from the individual women's organisations membership of the Mother's Union has decreased since the 1950s, falling from 492,000 in 1950 to 146,000 in 1995. A similar trend is evident in the National Federation of Women's Institutes, declining by more than 50 per cent from 447,000 in 1950 to 220,000 in 2003. The number of Townswomen's Guilds dropped from 2,028 in 1958 to 1,900 in 1998 and membership declined within the guilds from 75,000 in 1999 to 55,000 in 2003. The general decline in membership in women's organisations since the 1950s coincides with the growth of women's participation in the labour market. In 1950 around a third of women aged over

Table **7.10**

Membership of selected women's organisations, 1900 to 2003[1]

	Members of Mothers Union[2] (Thousands)	Members of Federation of Womens Institutes[3] (Thousands)	Number of Townswomen's Guilds[4]
1900	169.9	..	..
1911	362.6	..	..
1920	386.0	..	..
1930	510.1	291.6	4
1940	510.2	291.0	544
1950	492.2	446.7	..
1960	453.2	444.7	2,028
1970	334.1	436.4	..
1980	214.7	384.3	..
1990	173.4	318.7	..
1998	146.0	265.4	1,900
2003	..	220.0	..

1 Data for nearest year available given.
2 United Kingdom and Ireland.
3 England, Wales, Jersey, Guernsey and the Isle of Man.
4 United Kingdom.

Source: Organisations concerned; Halsey, A (ed) (2000) Twentieth Century British Social Trends

16 were in the workforce but by 2003 more than half had joined. It is likely that the growing number of women in paid employment has contributed to the decline in membership of women's organisations, with a reduction in the time available to participate.

Civic engagement

Civic engagement can be defined as voting in elections and other acts such as contacting a public official or attending a public meeting or demonstration. In recent years there has been a decline in voting in elections in the United Kingdom, while participation in other less conventional forms of civic engagement, such as attending a protest, has increased.

Voting

Voter turnout for the 2001 general election was 59 per cent, the lowest turnout for any post-war general election in the United Kingdom (Figure 7.11). Turnout peaked at the 1950 general election at 84 per cent. It then remained around 75 per cent until the early 1990s when it fell in both the 1997 and 2001 elections. The Electoral Commission found that there has also been a decline in turnout in local and European elections

in the last decade. On average only 33 per cent of the electorate voted at the local elections in 2002. The United Kingdom had one of the lowest turnout rates at the 2004 European Parliamentary elections, with an estimated 39 per cent. However, turnout had increased from 1999 when it was 24 per cent. Other countries with low turnouts included Portugal and the Netherlands, both at 39 per cent. The countries with the highest turnout were Belgium at 91 per cent where voting is mandatory and Italy at 73 per cent. In addition, some of the new member countries had much lower turnouts than the existing member states, for example, Slovakia (17 per cent) and Poland (21 per cent).

Figure **7.11**

Post-war turnout[1] for general elections
United Kingdom

Percentages

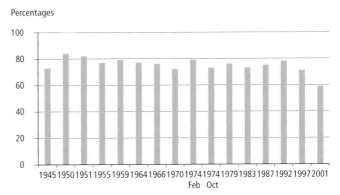

1 The number of votes cast as a percentage of the number of people on the electoral registers in force at the time of the elections.

Source: International Institute for Democracy and Electoral Assistance

Research by the Electoral Commission showed that certain groups of the electorate were less likely to vote than others. Turnout in Great Britain varied by age, gender, education, ethnicity, social class and area.[5] Young people aged between 18 and 24 were some of the least likely people to vote. It was estimated that in 2001 only 39 per cent of people aged 18 to 24 voted in the general election compared with 70 per cent of those aged 65. The reasons young people gave for not voting included disillusionment, apathy, alienation from politics, lack of knowledge and inconvenience of casting their vote.

Voter turnout also varied by employment status in the 2001 general election (Figure 7.12 – see overleaf). The economically inactive were the most likely to vote and the unemployed were the least likely. Seventy four per cent of economically inactive people voted compared with 48 per cent of unemployed people. For those in work, slightly more self-employed people voted compared with employed people: 71 per cent and 66 per cent respectively.

Figure **7.12**

Percentage of people who voted in the general election: by employment status, 2001

Great Britain

Percentages

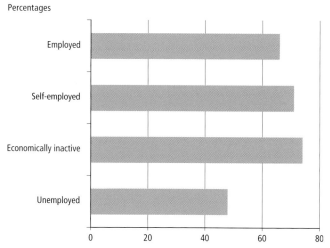

Source: British Household Panel Survey, Institute for Social and Economic Research

Other civic activities

While voter turnout has declined, the proportion of people taking part in other types of civic activities has increased. The Home Office Citizenship Survey (HOCS) in 2001 measured civic participation by asking respondents if they had engaged in any of a range of civic activities in the past 12 months. These activities included signing a petition, contacting a public official - a local councillor, a member of the Greater London Assembly, the National Assembly for Wales or a Member of Parliament; attending a public meeting or rally and taking part in a public demonstration or protest. The survey found that 38 per cent of adults in England and Wales had participated at least once in a civic activity in the past 12 months and that around three per cent participated in civic activities at least once a month. The most common activity was signing a petition (58 per cent). This was followed by contacting a public official working for a local council (38 per cent), contacting a local councillor (24 per cent), attending a public meeting or rally (18 per cent) and contacting a Member of Parliament (13 per cent).

The HOCS 2001 showed that men were slightly more likely than women to participate in civic activities. Rates of civic participation were also found to differ by ethnic group. Figure 7.13 shows that the White British (39 per cent) were the most likely to participate in a range of civic activities, closely followed by the White Irish (38 per cent), people from mixed race backgrounds (37 per cent) and Bangladeshi people (36 per cent). People of other Asian origin (25 per cent) and Chinese people (26 per cent) were the least likely to participate.

Figure **7.13**

Active participation in civic activities[1] by ethnic group, 2001

England & Wales

Percentages

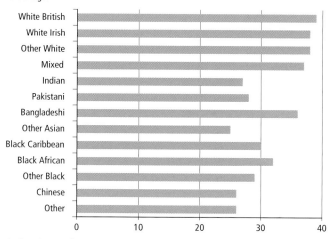

1 See Appendix, Part 7: Civic activities.

Source: Citizenship Survey, Home Office

Like participation in social organisations, the youngest and oldest age groups were the least likely to be involved in civic activities: 28 per cent of those aged 16 to 24 and 18 per cent of those aged over 85. In comparison, 45 per cent of those aged 45 to 54 had participated in civic activities at least once in the last 12 months, the age group with the highest proportion of participators.

Trends in civic participation

According to the BSA survey, with the exception of voting, civic participation in Great Britain increased from the mid-1980s to 2000 with a peak in the early 1990s (Table 7.14). Signing a petition has remained the most common form of participation throughout this time. It also showed the greatest proportionate increase from 34 per cent of adults aged 16 and over in 1986, to 53 per cent in 1991, when it then fell slightly to 43 per cent in 2002. The number of people who had contacted their MP rose from 11 per cent in 1986 to 17 per cent in 2002 and the percentage of people contacting a radio, television or newspaper or going on a protest or demonstration also increased from 1986.

Volunteering

The Government has stated an aim to promote the development of the voluntary and community sector and to encourage people to become actively involved in their communities, particularly in deprived areas, and have designed various schemes to achieve this. In 1999 the Millennium Volunteers scheme was established to encourage young people

Table 7.14

Active participation in civic activities[1]

England   Percentages

	1986	1989	1991	1994	2000	2002	Change 1986 to 2002
Signed a petition	34	41	53	39	42	43	+9
Contacted their MP	11	15	17	14	16	17	+6
Contacted radio, TV or newspaper	3	4	4	5	6	7	+4
Gone on a protest or demonstration	6	8	9	9	10	12	+6
Spoken to an influential person	3	3	5	3	4	6	+3
Contacted a government department[2]	3	3	4	3	4	..	..
Formed a group of like-minded people	2	3	2	3	2	2	0
Raised the issue in an organisation they already belong to	5	4	5	4	5	6	+1
None of these	56	48	37	53	47	46	-10

1 Figures do not add to 100 per cent as more than one response could be given.
2 Question not asked in 2002.

Source: British Social Attitudes Survey, National Centre for Social Research

aged 16 to 24 to volunteer in their local community. For older people the Home Office set up the Experience Corps in 2001, to encourage people aged 50 and over to volunteer and use their skills and experience to benefit others.

The HOCS in 2001 asked adults over the age of 16 in England and Wales whether they had volunteered informally at least once in the last 12 months. Informal volunteering was defined as giving unpaid help as an individual to others who were not members of the family. Examples of informal volunteering include giving advice to someone or doing shopping for someone. Sixty seven per cent of people had volunteered informally in the last 12 months. Each volunteer contributed on average 63 hours a year. In total 1.8 billion hours were volunteered which was worth around £18.2 billion based upon the national average hourly wage of £10.42 in 2001.[6]

The HOCS also asked people whether they had volunteered formally at least once in the last 12 months. Formal volunteering was defined as giving unpaid help through groups, clubs or organisations to benefit other people or the environment, such as raising or handling money or being a member of a committee. Fewer people volunteered formally than informally. However, people who volunteered formally contributed on average more time than people who volunteered informally. Thirty nine per cent of people volunteered formally in England and Wales but each formal volunteer contributed on average 106 hours a year (about three working weeks of 35 hours). In total 1.7 billion hours were volunteered formally, which was worth around £17.9 billion.[6]

The propensity to volunteer varied by ethnic group with people from White and Black ethnic groups more likely to be involved in informal and formal volunteering than Asian people (Figure 7.15). In contrast the Bangladeshi and Pakistani groups were the least likely to have volunteered informally. The pattern was similar for formal volunteering, although the Indian group was more likely to participate in these types of activities than other Asian groups.

Volunteers tended to have higher academic qualifications, be in higher socio-economic groups, be in employment and have the highest household incomes. People with a degree or

Figure 7.15

Volunteering: by ethnic group, 2001

England & Wales

Percentages

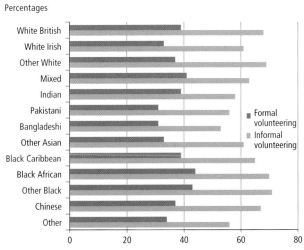

Source: Citizenship Survey, Home Office

postgraduate qualification were more likely to volunteer informally (79 per cent) and formally (57 per cent), than people with no qualifications (52 per cent and 23 per cent respectively). In terms of socio-economic group, three quarters of people in higher managerial occupations volunteered informally and half volunteered formally. This is compared with just over two fifths of people who volunteered informally and nearly a fifth who volunteered formally in the never worked and the long term unemployed socio-economic group. Seventy two per cent of employed people volunteered informally, as did 64 per cent of unemployed people. People with higher household incomes were also more likely to volunteer (Figure 7.16). For those living in households with gross annual incomes of £75,000 or more, 57 per cent had volunteered formally. However, for those living in households with an annual income under £10,000, around 30 per cent had volunteered formally. A similar pattern of participation increasing with income was shown also for informal volunteering. Those earning £50,000 to £74,999 were the most likely to volunteer informally at 80 per cent.

Of those people who volunteered informally, the activities they were most likely to engage in were giving advice to someone (46 per cent) and looking after a property or a pet for someone who was away (41 per cent) (Table 7.17). The types of activities people did varied by sex and ethnic group. Men were four times more likely than women to decorate or do home or car

repairs for others. While women were more likely than men to baby sit or care for children, keep in touch with someone who has difficulty getting out, do the shopping for someone, collect pensions or pay bills and sit with or provide personal care for someone who was sick or frail.

Figure **7.16**

Volunteering: by household income[1], 2001

England & Wales

Percentages

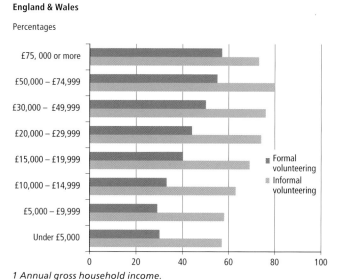

1 Annual gross household income.

Source: Citizenship Survey, Home Office

Table **7.17**

Informal volunteering[1]: by sex, 2001[2]

England & Wales

Percentages

	Males	Females	All
Giving advice to someone	48	44	46
Looking after a property or a pet for someone who is away	39	43	41
Transporting or escorting someone	32	30	31
Babysitting or caring for children	19	39	29
Keeping in touch with someone who has difficulty getting out and about	25	32	28
Doing shopping, collecting pensions or paying bills for someone	20	31	26
Writing letters or filling in forms for someone	22	24	23
Cooking, cleaning, laundry, gardening or other routine household jobs for someone	17	17	17
Decorating or doing any kind of home or car repairs for someone	25	6	16
Representing someone	7	5	6
Sitting with or providing personal care for someone who is sick or frail	3	7	5
Any other activities	2	2	2

1 Defined as giving unpaid help as an individual to others who are not members of the family.
2 In the last 12 months.

Source: Citizenship Survey, Home Office

People who volunteered formally were most likely to engage in raising or handling money (56 per cent) or organising or helping to run an activity or event (54 per cent) (Table 7.18). White and Asian people were more likely to raise or handle money than Black people. White people were the most likely to organise or help run an activity or event, lead a group or be a member of a committee and provide transport compared with other ethnic groups. Black people, however, were more likely than White or Asian people to give advice or counselling and visit or befriend people.

Women were more likely than men to volunteer in activities connected to children's education and schools, religion, the elderly, health, disability and social welfare. Men were more likely than women to engage in social activities such as sports and exercise, hobbies, social clubs and trade union activities. Black and Asian people were around three times as likely as White people to be engaged in religious activities. In contrast White people were more likely than Black and Asian people to be engaged in sporting activities, hobbies and social clubs. Eight per cent of Black people were involved in justice and human rights campaigns, double the proportion of White and Asian people.

Social networks

Social networks can be defined as the personal relationships that connect individuals to one another and to society as a whole. These ties may be with family members, friends or neighbours, or within other more formal settings such as social organisations. Regular contact with friends and relatives is not

only important in itself but it has other benefits. Friends and family can be an important source of support in stressful times, they can also provide financial help and transport. However, certain groups of people have very limited social networks and have infrequent contact with other people outside of the home.

Much of people's social contact with others occurs in the home. In recent years there have been several notable changes in household composition, with fewer people living in traditional family units (couple families with dependent children) and a rise in the proportion of single and lone-parent households. Data from the Census and the Labour Force Survey indicated that the proportion of single person households in Great Britain increased from 18 per cent of households in 1971 to 29 per cent in 2003. The greatest increase has been among men under the age of 65 living alone. During the same period there was a decline in the proportion of large households. The proportion of households made up of five or more people fell from 14 per cent in 1971 to seven per cent in 2003. The proportion of households that were lone-parent families with dependent children doubled between 1971 and 1991, from three to six per cent and has remained around this level up to 2003. Lone parenthood has been particularly high among Black families. According to the 2001 Census 43 per cent of Black families were lone-parent families, compared with 22 per cent of White and 11 per cent of Asian families.

In 2000 the General Household Survey (GHS) asked adults aged 16 and over in Great Britain how frequently they were in contact with friends and relatives who lived outside of the

Table **7.18**

Formal volunteering[1]: by ethnic group, 2001

England & Wales   Percentages

	White	Asian	Black	All
Raising or handling money	56	52	40	56
Organising or helping to run an activity or event	55	44	47	54
Giving other practical help (direct services)	35	32	33	35
Leading a group/being a member of a committee	35	23	28	34
Giving advice/information/counselling	28	31	41	29
Providing transport/driving	27	19	16	26
Visiting/befriending people	21	31	36	22
Secretarial, administration or clerical work	18	12	14	18
Representing	16	15	16	16
Campaigning	13	11	10	12
Any other help	7	8	11	7

1 Defined as giving unpaid help through groups, clubs or organisations to benefit others or the environment in the last 12 months.

Source: Citizenship Survey, Home Office

household, either in person or on the telephone, and how many close friends and family members lived nearby. People tended to speak to relatives on the phone more frequently than they spoke to friends but saw friends more regularly than they saw relatives.

People with educational qualifications were less likely to have regular contact with relatives or have close relatives living nearby than people with no qualifications. Fifty nine per cent of people with qualifications above A-level had no close relatives living nearby compared with 31 per cent of people with no qualifications. Those with qualifications above A-level were also less likely to have close friends living nearby. Thirty one per cent of people with qualifications had no close friends nearby compared with 26 per cent of people with no qualifications. This reflects the likelihood of greater mobility among people with higher academic qualifications.

Length of residence in an area affects how often people meet up with their relatives and how many close relatives and friends they have living nearby. The GHS defines a satisfactory friendship or relative network as seeing or speaking to friends or relatives at least once a week and having at least one close friend or relative living nearby. The longer people have lived in an area, the more established their social networks are. Seventy two per cent of people who had lived in an area for more than twenty years had a satisfactory friendship network

and 65 per cent had a satisfactory relatives network (Figure 7.19). In contrast, of those who had lived in an area for less than five years, 53 per cent had satisfactory friendship networks and 34 per cent had satisfactory relatives networks. People who had lived in an area for less than five years were twice as likely to have no close friends or relatives living nearby and twice as likely not to see relatives daily than people who had lived in an area for 20 years or more.

Young adults aged 16 to 29 had the most active social networks, as indicated by the GHS. They were more likely than older adults to phone friends and see them regularly and have at least five close friends living nearby. Findings from the BSA survey suggested that friendship networks also varied by income, with people living in poorer households having fewer friends than those living in more affluent households.[7]

There are substantial regional differences in the proportions of people with satisfactory friendship and relative networks (Figure 7.20). People living in Wales and Scotland were more likely to see friends and relatives regularly, speak to them on the phone daily and have five close friends or relatives living nearby than people in England. Twenty three per cent of people in Wales and 21 per cent of people in Scotland saw relatives daily compared with 13 per cent of people in England. Within England, those living in the North East were the most likely to have a satisfactory friendship and relatives network,

Figure **7.19**

Whether has satisfactory friendship or relative network[1]: by length of residence in the area, 2000

Great Britain

Percentages

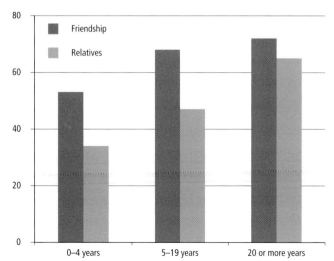

1   *Those described as having a satisfactory friendship or relatives network were those people who saw or spoke to friends or relatives at least once a week and had at least one close friend or relative who lived nearby.*

Source: General Household Survey, Office for National Statistics

Figure **7.20**

Whether has satisfactory friendship or relative network[1]: by region, 2000

Great Britain

Percentages

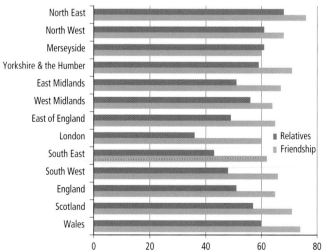

1   *Those described as having a satisfactory friendship or relatives network were those people who saw or spoke to friends or relatives at least once a week and had at least one close friend or relative who lived nearby.*

Source: General Household Survey, Office for National Statistics

while people living in London and the South East were the least likely. Those living in London were considerably less likely to have a satisfactory relatives network than all other regions. Only seven per cent of people in London saw relatives each day compared with 26 per cent of people in the North East.

Neighbourliness and reciprocity

Neighbourliness and reciprocity are other forms of social interaction, which can have an important impact on quality of life and social cohesion. The GHS defines neighbourliness as knowing and trusting neighbours, looking out for each other and giving and receiving favours from neighbours. Reciprocity is measured by whether people look out for their neighbours and do favours for them. Forty six per cent of people said they knew most or many people in their neighbourhood and 27 per cent reported speaking to their neighbours daily in Great Britain in 2000. More people said they trusted their neighbours (58 per cent) than said they knew their neighbours (46 per cent), which suggests that some people have a generalised trust, in that they trust people they do not personally know.

Younger people aged 16 to 29 were the least likely to know, speak to or trust their neighbours. Younger people also had lower levels of reciprocity, in terms of giving and receiving favours from neighbours and whether they thought neighbours looked out for one another. Fifty seven per cent of younger people had done a favour for a neighbour in the past six months. Older people were the most likely to do a favour for a neighbour, 82 per cent of people aged 60 to 69 said they had done a favour for a neighbour in the past six months.

Evidence suggests there is a relationship between neighbourliness and those characteristics which reflect disadvantage in England, such as socio-economic group, tenure and education. People who are more disadvantaged were generally more likely to know and speak to their neighbours but less likely to trust or have a reciprocal relationship with them. Similarly, comparison by socio-economic group revealed that people in manual occupations were more likely to know and speak to their neighbours than people in non-manual occupations but were less likely to trust them or have done and received favours from them. People in the most deprived wards were less trusting of their neighbours and less likely to feel that people in their area looked out for one another than people in less deprived wards (Figure 7.21). Forty per cent of people in the most deprived wards trusted most or many of their neighbours compared with 73 per cent of people in the least deprived wards. However, people in the most deprived wards were more likely to speak to their neighbours daily (33 per cent) than people in the least deprived wards (19 per cent).

Figure **7.21**

Neighbourliness: by Index of Multiple Deprivation, 2000[1]

England

Percentages

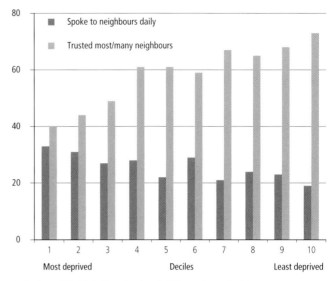

1 Index of Multiple Deprivation; 2000 wards, ranked from top to bottom and divided into 10 equal percentile groups.

Source: General Household Survey, Office for National Statistics

Social support

The family tends to be the main source of help for the majority of people in times of crisis. For instance, when asked who they would call upon if they were ill in bed or if they were in financial difficulty and needed to borrow £100, most people said they would turn to their spouse or partner or another relative outside of the household. One exception was if people needed a lift somewhere urgently, in this case they were more likely to ask a friend for help. Over half of respondents (58 per cent) had at least five people they could turn to in a serious personal crisis. Eighteen per cent had less than three people they could turn to and were thus described by the GHS as having low social support.

People in owner-occupied accommodation had greater social support in terms of having more people to call upon for help and more people who lived locally than people living in rented accommodation. People living in privately rented accommodation had better access to financial support and more people to turn to in a serious personal crisis than social renters. Seventeen per cent of owner occupiers and 14 per cent of private renters had at least three sources of financial help, compared with only seven per cent of social renters.

Comparison by household type showed that couples had more social support than single parents, one person and non-related households. Single person households had the least social support in contrast to all the other household types. When in financial difficulty only two per cent of one-person households had three sources of informal help compared with 20 per cent of couples with dependent children and 21 per cent of couples with non-dependent children. Couples (with dependent or non-dependent children) were also more likely to have at least five sources of social support than one-person and lone-parent households.

Certain groups of people were more likely to have someone to rely on to help find work than others. The BHPS in 2001 asked whether there was anyone they could rely on outside of the household if they needed help finding a job for themselves or a family member. Non-related households (72 per cent) in Great Britain and lone parents with dependent children (68 per cent) were the most likely to have someone outside of the household who could help them find a job. Single person households (50 per cent) and couples with no children (54 per cent) were the least likely to have someone who could help find a job. Other research supports this finding. A survey of lone parents conducted as part of the New Deal evaluation states that 30 per cent of lone parents interviewed had found their current job through family and friends, compared with 10 per cent who found employment through a Jobcentre.[8]

Barriers to participation

Some people lack, or are denied access to, social networks and activities, such as visiting friends and family or being a member of a club, which are common social activities considered necessities by the majority of the population. There are many reasons for non-participation. The main barriers are a lack of resources such as money and time, and personal circumstances such as caring responsibilities. Fear of crime, health status or disability, access to transport, and lack of information regarding opportunities to join clubs or volunteer and of the need for help were also considered as being barriers to participation. Personal efficacy has been suggested as another reason for non-participation. People who had a sense of their own personal worth and felt able to influence outcomes or felt that institutions were responsive to their intervention were more likely to participate than those who did not.[9]

The 1999 Poverty and Social Exclusion (PSE) survey asked adults aged 16 and over in Great Britain which social activities, from a selection of fifteen such as having a hobby or visiting friends or family in hospital, they considered were necessities for life. Table 7.22 shows the reasons people gave for not participating in these activities, which were considered by many to be a necessity. Lack of money (47 per cent) was cited most often as the factor preventing people from participating.

Table **7.22**

Factors preventing participation in common social activities[1], 1999

Great Britain	Percentages
	Non-participation [2]
Can't afford to	47
Not interested	44
Lack of time due to childcare responsibilities	18
Too old, ill, sick or disabled	14
Lack of time due to paid work	14
No one to go out with (social)	6
No vehicle/poor public transport	5
Lack of time due to other caring responsibilities	4
Fear of burglary or vandalism	3
Fear of personal attack	3
Can't go out due to other caring responsibilities	2
Problems with physical access	1
Feel unwelcome (eg due to disability, ethnicity, gender, age)	1
None of these	8

1 For the full list of social activities used in the Poverty and Social Exclusion Survey questionnaire see Appendix, Part 7: Social activities.
2 Includes multiple responses.

Source: Poverty and Social Exclusion Survey of Britain, Joseph Rowntree Foundation

Unemployed people (59 per cent) and people living in workless households (50 per cent) were the most likely to say that they could not participate in two or more social activities because they could not afford to. Households with children and people aged between 16 to 34 also participated less because of lack of money, with 40 per cent and 36 per cent of people respectively, saying that they could not afford to participate in two or more social activities.

The most frequently cited barrier to participation after a lack of money, was a lack of interest or inclination (44 per cent). This suggested that many people chose not to participate rather than being prevented from participating by external factors. Other barriers to participation included lack of time due to childcare responsibilities, paid work, sickness or disability.

Factors such as fear of crime and concern for personal safety can prevent people from leaving their homes, particularly after dark, and thus reduce their level of activity. In more extreme cases they can be left totally excluded from social activities. Thirty per cent of people in the PSE survey felt unsafe walking alone after dark and three per cent said that fear of personal attack prevented them participating in common social activities. Those most likely to feel unsafe were women, people aged over 65, those not in paid work and those living in workless households.

Health status also affected whether people participated or not, with poor health and disability acting as a barrier for many people. The BHPS in 2001 showed that of those people who said their health was excellent, 52 per cent were active in any of a range of social, political or community organisations, compared with 35 per cent of people who said their health was very poor. Disabled people were also less likely to participate in social activities. Thirty-seven per cent of disabled people were active in an organisation compared with 47 per cent of non-disabled people.

Transport was also a major barrier to participation for some groups. People without cars were twice as likely as those with cars to report that transport was a barrier to participation in a range of social and cultural activities.[10] Eighteen per cent of people without cars said they had trouble seeing friends and family compared with eight per cent of people with cars. A lack of transport was a particular problem for younger and older people. The main issues identified by elderly people were difficulties accessing public transport due to inadequate crossing facilities and problems boarding or alighting buses and trains, concerns over safety, affordability and availability. Many elderly people do not have access to a car and therefore they are restricted in choice of destination, flexibility and spontaneity of travel.[11] The Commission for Integrated Transport found that for younger people aged 16 to 24, 39 per cent stated that better public transport would improve their social lives.[12]

According to HOCS in 2001 the main barrier to informal volunteering identified by adults in Great Britain who had never volunteered, or who had volunteered infrequently, was time commitments (Table 7.23). This was followed by lack of awareness of the need for help and of opportunities to help, personal circumstances such as looking after children, caring or other family responsibilities and health, and work or educational commitments. Women were more likely than men to report that personal circumstances prevented them volunteering informally: 22 per cent compared with 14 per cent respectively. People aged between 25 and 49 were more likely than other ages to identify time commitments as a barrier to volunteering. Those aged over 65 were more likely than those aged between 16 and 64 to report personal circumstances as a barrier to informal volunteering.

A lack of time was also the main factor that prevented people from volunteering formally in the HOCS survey (34 per cent) (Table 7.24 – see overleaf). After time commitments the most frequently mentioned barriers were personal circumstances and educational or work commitments, each by a quarter of people, similar to informal volunteering. Again women were more likely than men to report personal circumstances as a barrier but men were more likely to mention work or educational commitments.

There was also variation between ethnic groups. Twenty seven per cent of White people identified personal circumstances as preventing them volunteering formally compared with 20 per cent of Black people. Black people (15 per cent) were more likely to mention lack of awareness of the need for help and of opportunities to help than White (8 per cent) or Asian (10 per cent) people.

Table **7.23**

Barriers to involvement in informal volunteering[1]: by sex and by age, 2001

England & Wales   Percentages

		Sex		Age					
	All	Males	Females	16–24	25–34	35–49	50–64	65–74	75 and over
Time commitments	31	32	31	30	40	37	29	..	..
Lack of awareness of need for help/opportunities to help	27	28	27	28	28	25	29	34	17
Personal circumstances	18	14	22	9	13	16	18	37	58
Working or educational commitments	14	15	13	20	14	16	14	..	..
Community integration issues	6	7	6	..	6	6	7	..	..
Personality issues	2	..	2	..	..	..	..	..	..

1 *Barriers to involvement or greater involvement. Informal volunteering was defined as giving unpaid help as an individual to others who are not members of the family.*

Source: Citizenship Survey, Home Office

Table **7.24**

Barriers to involvement in formal volunteering[1]: by sex and by ethnic group, 2001

England & Wales

Percentages

	All	Sex		Ethnic group		
		Males	Females	White	Asian	Black
Time commitments	34	34	35	35	31	32
Personal circumstances	26	20	32	27	24	20
Working or educational commitments	25	28	23	25	26	20
Lack of awareness of need for help/opportunities to help	8	10	7	8	10	15
Personality issues	5	6	4	6	..	7
Community integration issues	2	..	2	2	4	..

1 Barriers to involvement or greater involvement. Formal volunteering was defined as giving unpaid help through groups, clubs or organisations to benefit others or the environment.

Source: Citizenship Survey, Home Office

People were also asked what the main incentives were to overcome these barriers. People who said they would like to volunteer or to spend more time volunteering informally indicated that the main incentive was knowing someone in need of help (59 per cent) and being asked directly to get involved (52 per cent). Regarding formal volunteering, the main incentives identified were being asked directly to get involved (44 per cent) and getting involved with friends or family (40 per cent). Twenty five per cent of people also said improving skills or getting qualifications was an incentive.

Conclusion

Social participation in clubs and organisations, contact with friends and family and engagement in civic activities are important to people's quality of life and can play a part in improving health, reducing crime and building cohesive communities.

However, certain groups of people, particularly those from disadvantaged backgrounds, are more likely to be excluded from participating in social and civic activities and have fewer social networks outside of the household. People with lower or no educational qualifications, those working in lower paid occupations, the unemployed and lone parents are less likely to participate, than those from more advantaged backgrounds. Certain minority ethnic groups, particularly Bangladeshi and Pakistani, are also less likely to be participate than other ethnic groups. Young people and elderly people are less likely to join in the activities of social organisations or participate in civic life. However, young people have the most active friendship and relative networks compared with other age groups.

Lack of resources such as time and money was the most frequently cited barrier to participation in social and civic activities. Other barriers to participation included mobilisation, poor health or a disability and not having own transport. Lack of information regarding opportunities and lack of awareness of the need for help also prevented people from joining in. The final reason for non-engagement may concern individuals' sense of personal efficacy. People who thought their contribution would have an impact were more likely to participate than those who thought they could not make any difference.

References

1. Department for Culture, Media and Sport (1999) Arts and Sport, PAT 10 Report.

2. Ferri E, Bynner J and Wadsworth M (2003) Changing Britain, Changing Lives, Three generations at the turn of the century, Institute of Education, University of London.

3. Catan L (2002) Youth, Citizenship and Social Change, Economic and Social Research Council, http://www.tsa.uk.com/YCSC/index.html

4. Johnston M and Jowell R (2001) British Social Attitudes: the 18th Report. 'How robust is British civil society?' National Centre for Social Research. London: Sage

5. Electoral Commission (2002) Voter engagement and young people, Research Report, http:// www.electoralcommission.org.uk (archive)

6. Attwood C, Singh G, Prime D and Creasey R (2003) 2001 Home Office Citizenship Survey: people, families and communities, Home Office Research Study, London.

7. Park A and Roberts C (2003) *British Social Attitudes: the 20th Report. 'The ties that bind.'* National Centre for Social Research. London. Sage

8. Hales J, Lessof C, Roth W, Gloyer M, Shaw A, Millar J, Barnes M, Elias P, Hasluck C, McKnight A and Green A (2000) *Evaluation of the New Deal for Lone Parents,* DSS Research Report 108

9. Pattie C, Seyd P and Whiteley P (Forthcoming) *Citizenship in Britain: Values, Participation and Democracy,* Cambridge University Press

10. Ruston D (2002) Difficulty in Accessing Key Services, *http://www.statistics.gov.uk/downloads/theme_social/access_key_services/access_to_services.pdf*

11. Department for Transport (2000) Older people: Their transport needs and requirements, *http://www.dft.gov.uk/stellent/groups/dft _mobility/documents/page/dft_mobility_ 506792.hcsp*

12. Commission for Integrated Transport (CfIT) (2001) Public Attitudes to Transport in England (cited in social Exclusion Unit, *Making the Connections: Final Report on Transport and Social Exclusion,* 2003)

Appendix

Appendix

Part 1: Symbols, conventions and abbreviations

Symbols and conventions

Rounding of figures. In tables where figures have been rounded to the nearest final digit, there may be an apparent discrepancy between the sum of the constituent items and the total as shown.

Billion. This term is used to represent a thousand million.

Provisional and estimated data. Some data for the latest year (and occasionally for earlier years) are provisional or estimated. To keep footnotes to a minimum, these have not been indicated; source departments will be able to advise if revised data are available.

Non-calendar years

Financial year – eg 1 April 2001 to 31 March 2002 would be shown as 2001/02

Academic year – eg September 2000/July 2001 would be shown as 2000/01

Combined years – eg 2000-02 shows data for more than one year that have been combined

Data covering more than one year – eg 1998, 1999 and 2000 would be shown as 1998 to 2000

Units on tables. Where one unit predominates it is shown at the top of the table. All other units are shown against the relevant row or column. Figures are shown in italics when they represent percentages.

Dependent children. Those aged under 16, or single people aged 16 to 18 and in full-time education.

Symbols. The following symbols have been used throughout the report:

..	not available
.	not applicable
-	negligible (*less than half the final digit shown*)
0	nil

Abbreviations

API	Age participation index
BCS	British Crime Survey
BHPS	British Household Panel Survey
BSA	British Social Attitudes survey
CHS	Continuous Household Survey
CIS-R	Clinical Interview Schedule
DfES	Department for Education and Skills
DfT	Department for Transport
DiPTAC	Disabled Persons Transport Advisory Committee
DTI	Department for Trade and Industry
DWP	Department for Work and Pensions
ECHP	European Community Household Panel Survey
EFS	Expenditure and Food Survey
EHCS	English House Condition Survey
EMA	Educational Maintenance Allowance
EPPE	Effective Provision of Pre-school Education (Project)
FE	Further education
FRS	Family Resources Survey
FSM	Free school meals
GCSE	General Certificate of Secondary Education
GHS	General Household Survey
GNVQ	General National Vocational Qualification
GP	General Practitioner
HE	Higher education
HSE	Health Survey for England
HOCS	Home Office Citzenship Survey
ICT	Information and communication technology
IFS	Institute of Fiscal Studies
IHD	Ischaemic heart disease
ILO	International Labour Organisation
LEA	Local education authorities
LFS	Labour Force Survey
LLTI	Limiting long-term illness
NALS	National Adult Learning Survey
NES	New Earnings Survey
NS-SEC	National Statistics Socio-Economic Classification
NTS	National Travel Survey
NVQ	National vocational qualification
ODPM	Office of the Deputy Prime Minister
OECD	Organisation for Economic Co-operation and Development
OfA	Opportunity for All
ONS	Office for National Statistics
PISA	Programme for International Student Assessment
PLASC	Pupil Level Annual School Census
PSE	Poverty and Social Exclusion Survey
SCE(S)	Scottish Certificate of Education: Standard Grade
SEH	Survey English Housing
SEN	Special education needs
SEU	Social Exclusion Unit
YCS	Youth Cohort Study

Part 2: Education, training and skills

British birth cohort studies

There are four national birth cohort studies that collect information about people at birth and then continue to study these same people periodically over time. The Medical Research Council's National Survey of Health and Development began in 1946, and was followed by the National Child Development Study in 1958, the 1970 British Cohort Study in 1970 and the Millennium Cohort Study in 2000.

GCE A level points score system

The A level points score system was developed to help with the presentation of statistics and was used by the Universities & Colleges Admissions Service (UCAS) for student admissions to universities and colleges until 2002, when it was superseded by the UCAS Tariff. See *www.ucas.co.uk* for more details. GCE A level points score system: 10 points for an A grade, 8 for a B, 6 for a C, 4 for a D and 2 for an E.

National Curriculum

The *Education Act 2002* extended the National Curriculum for England to include a foundation stage. It has six areas of learning, namely: personal, social and emotional development; communication, language and literacy; mathematical development; knowledge and understanding of the world; physical development; and creative development.

Under the *Education Reform Act (1988)* a National Curriculum has been progressively introduced into primary and secondary schools in England and Wales. This consists of English (or the option of Welsh as a first language in Wales), mathematics and science. The second level of curriculum additionally comprises the so-called 'foundation' subjects, such as history, geography, art, music, information technology, design and technology and physical education (and Welsh as a second language in Wales).

Measurable targets have been defined for four key stages, corresponding to ages 7, 11, 14 and 16. Pupils are assessed formally at the ages of 7, 11 and 14 by their teachers and by national tests in the core subjects of English, mathematics and science (and in Welsh speaking schools in Wales, Welsh). Sixteen-year-olds are assessed by means of the GCSE examination. Statutory authorities have been set up for England and for Wales to advise government on the National Curriculum and promote curriculum development generally. Statutory assessment at the end of Key Stage 1 in Wales in 2002 was by means of teacher assessment only.

In Wales the National Curriculum Tests/Tasks were discontinued in 2002 following the outcome of the public consultation on proposed changes to the assessment arrangements contained in *The Learning Country – A Comprehensive Education and Lifelong Learning Programme to 2010 in Wales.*

Northern Ireland has its own common curriculum which is similar but not identical to the National Curriculum in England and Wales. Assessment arrangements in Northern Ireland became statutory from September 1996 and Key Stage 1 pupils are assessed at the age of 8. Pupils in Northern Ireland are not assessed in science at Key Stages 1 and 2.

In Scotland there is no statutory national curriculum. Pupils aged 5 to 14 study a broad curriculum based on national guidelines which set out the aims of study, the ground to be covered and the way the pupils' learning should be assessed and reported. Progress is measured by attainment of six levels based on the expectation of the performance of the majority of pupils on completion of certain stages between the ages of 5 and 14: Primary 3 (age 7/8), Primary 4 (age 8/9), Primary 7 (age 11/12) and Secondary 2 (age 13/14). It is recognised that pupils learn at different rates and some will reach the various levels before others.

The curriculum areas are: language; mathematics; environmental studies; expressive arts; and religious and moral education with personal and social development and health education. Though school curricula are the responsibility of education authorities and individual head teachers, in practice almost all 14- to 16- year-olds study mathematics, English, science, a modern foreign language, a social subject, physical education, religious and moral education, technology and a creative and aesthetic subject.

England	Attainment expected
Key Stage 1	Level 2 or above
Key Stage 2	Level 4 or above
Key Stage 3	Level 5/6 or above
Key Stage 4	GCSE

National Vocational Qualification (NVQ) levels

Qualifications are often expressed as being equivalent to a particular NVQ level so that comparisons can be made more easily. An NVQ level 5 is equivalent to a Higher Degree. An NVQ level 4 is equivalent to a First Degree, a HND or HNC, a BTEC Higher Diploma, an RSA Higher Diploma, a nursing qualification or other Higher Education. An NVQ level 3 is equivalent to two A levels, an advanced GNVQ, an RSA advanced diploma, a City & Guilds advanced craft, an OND or ONC or a BTEC National Diploma. An NVQ level 2 is equivalent to five GCSEs at grades A* to C, an Intermediate GNVQ, an

RSA diploma, a City and Guilds craft or a BTEC first or general diploma.

OECD PISA study (*www.oecd.org*)

The Programme for International Student Assessment (PISA) is a collaborative study among 28 member countries of the Organisation for Economic Co-operation and Development (OECD), plus Hungary, Latvia, Liechtenstein and the Russian Federation. Its main purpose is to assess the knowledge and skills of 15 year olds in three broad areas of literacy: reading, mathematics and science. PISA was carried out in 32 countries in 2000 when the main focus was on reading literacy, and will be repeated in 2003 and 2006, when the main focuses will be literacy in mathematics and science respectively. ONS carried out the study in England and Northern Ireland. The Scottish Executive carried out a separate study in Scotland. In each domain of literacy, a student's score is expressed as a number of points on a scale, and shows the highest difficulty of task that the student is likely to be able to complete. The scales are constructed so that the average score for students from all countries participating in PISA 2000 is 500 and its standard deviation is 100 – that is, about two thirds of students internationally score between 400 and 600. Each country contributes equally to this average irrespective of its size. Differences in PISA scores between countries should not be taken to result solely from differences in schooling, but rather from differences in the cumulative effect of learning experiences, because learning starts before school and occurs in different institutional and out-of-school settings. It should be noted that some of these differences are due to the standard errors around the estimates.

School types

Comprehensive schools largely admit pupils without reference to ability or aptitude and cater for all children in a neighbourhood. Selective schools, such as Grammar schools, select all or almost all of their pupils by reference to higher academic ability. Modern schools have no current statutory definition. Some schools describe themselves as 'modern' or 'secondary modern' but the use of this label varies, most commonly in areas with selective schools, and can depend on the views of the governing body. Comprehensive, modern and selective schools are all maintained and funded by local education authorities and central government. Other maintained schools include community, foundation, special and hospital schools and pupil referral units. Independent schools are schools that are usually funded by fee-paying students and are not maintained by the local authority or central government.

Skills for life national standards framework

A key element of the Government's Skills for Life strategy is the framework of a set of national standards for literacy and numeracy. Each set of standards consists of a framework which presents each skill at Entry level (divided into three sub-levels), Level 1 and Level 2 or above. A similar structure has been adopted for ICT skills.

Social and civic participation

Social participation represents involvement in clubs, groups and organisations. Civic participation represents a range of activities including: contacting an official or MP, attending a public meeting or rally, signing a petition, and taking part in a demonstration or protest. Informal volunteering is defined as giving unpaid help as an individual to others who are not members of the family. Formal volunteering is defined as giving unpaid help through groups, clubs or organisations to benefit others or the environment.

Socio-economic classification

National Statistics socio-economic classification

From April 2001 the National Statistics socio-economic classification (NS-SEC) was introduced for all official statistics and surveys. It has replaced social class based on occupation and socio-economic groups (SEG). Full details can be found in *The National Statistics Socio-Economic Classification User Manual 2002*, ONS 2002.

Descriptive definition NS-SEC categories:

Combined NS-SEC Category Description	NS-SEC Category	NS-SEC category Description
Managerial and professional occupations	L1, L2	Large employers and higher managerial occupations
	L3	Higher professional occupations
	L4, L5, L6	Lower managerial and professional occupations
Intermediate occupations	L7	Intermediate occupations
	L8, L9	Small employers and own account workers
Routine and manual occupations	L10, L11	Lower supervisory and technical occupations
	L12	Semi-routine occupations
	L13	Routine occupations

Excluded when the classification is collapsed into its analytical classes	L14	Never worked and long-term unemployed
	L15	Full time students
	L16	Occupation not stated or inadequately described
	L17	Not classifiable for other reasons

This results in the exclusion of those who have never worked and the long-term unemployed, in addition to the groups mentioned in the table. Since the introduction of the NS-SEC, the manual group in the DH target on smoking has been replaced by routine and manual class (see Figure 6.5).

The full version of NS-SEC is based on occupation, employment status and size of organisation (as collected by ONS surveys). However, for vital events such as births and deaths, size of organisation is not collected by registrars. Therefore, a version referred to as 'Reduced NS-SEC' is used, based on occupation and employment status only.

For years prior to 2001, an approximate version of NS-SEC (NS-SEC 90) is used. This is because the derivation of NS-SEC uses occupation coded in a version of the ONS Standard Occupational Classification introduced in 2001, while NS-SEC 90 uses occupation coded in the previous occupational classification and has some differences in the coding rules applied to employment status.

For births and infant deaths, father's occupation and employment status (e.g. employee, self-employed) are used to derive NS-SEC. Consequently only births within marriage, or births outside marriage registered by both parents, are included in the analysis by NS-SEC.

Infant mortality data presented in this report relate to 12 September 2002. Therefore, these figures may differ slightly from those published elsewhere.

Registrar General's Social Class

Registrar General's Social Class based on occupation has been the used in the United Kingdom since its first appearance in the *Registrar General's Annual Report* of 1911. Social class is derived from the individual's current or former occupation (see below) and employment status (such as employee, manager, or self-employed). For some occupations the size of the workplace is also used when that information is available, such as in the Census. Social class can be grouped into non-manual or manual occupations.

Registrar General's Social Class – examples of occupations:

Non-manual

I	Professional	Doctors, lawyers, charted accountants, professionally qualified engineers
II	Intermediate	Managers, school teachers, journalists
IIIN	Skilled non-manual	Clerks, cashiers, retail staff

Manual

IIIM	Skilled manual	Supervisors of manual workers, plumbers, electricians, bus drivers
IV	Partly skilled	Warehousemen, security guards, machine tool operators, care assistants
V	Unskilled	Labourers, cleaners and messengers

Registrar General's socio-economic group

Registrar General's socio-economic grouping (SEG) is the occupational classification which has been used on the General Household Survey. For persons aged 16 or over, including full-time students with employment experience, socio-economic group corresponds to their own present job, or, for those not currently working, to their last job, regardless of sex or marital status. Persons whose occupation was inadequately described, the Armed Forces and full-time students are excluded. The groups have been collapsed into non-manual and manual. The non-manual category comprises of SEGs 1-6 and 13, the manual category comprises of SEGs 7-12, 14 and 15.

Descriptive definition	SEG number
Professional	3,4
Employers and managers	1,2,13
Intermediate non-manual	5
Junior non-manual	6
Skilled manual (including foremen and supervisors) and own account non-professional	8,9,12,14
Semi-skilled manual and personal service	7,10,15
Unskilled manual	11

Part 3: Work

Disability

The Labour Force Survey (LFS) definition of current long-term disability includes all those who report having a work-limiting disability or a current disability covered by the Disability Discrimination Act (DDA). This definition gives the most comprehensive coverage of disability.

Ethnic group classifications

The National Statistics interim standard classification of ethnic groups is used. These data have had 'Other' specified answers re-coded into the appropriate category according to the 2001 Census of Population schema. Data for periods prior to this used the old classification. No comparison should be made between the two classifications because not only are the categories different, but the questions and coding of answers underlying the data are also very different.

These data are presented for Great Britain only and exclude Northern Ireland. Detailed level ethnicity questions are not asked of the White group in Northern Ireland. The sub-categories British and Other White will therefore not sum to the White total.

Experimental time-series data

The Office for National Statistics has produced a set of historical estimates on an experimental basis covering the period 1971–91, which are fully consistent with the post-1992 Labour Force Survey data. The data cover headline measures of employment, unemployment, economic activity and hours worked.

Headline UK labour market figures for employment and unemployment are taken from the LFS. The definitions used in the LFS are based on internationally agreed standards set by the International Labour Organisation. These definitions are designed to ensure international comparability of data.

However, LFS data are generally only available back to 1979. In addition, there have been a number of definitional changes over the years since the LFS was introduced. As a result, fully consistent survey data are only available back to 1992. This is insufficient for many users who need longer time series for modelling, and it makes comparisons over time difficult.

The historical estimates have been updated to take on board the full census reweighting of the LFS microdata (March 2004) and the latest revisions to workforce jobs (April 2004). Their status will be reviewed to decide whether they should remain as experimental statistics or whether they should become National Statistics.

For further information see: *http://www.statistics.gov.uk/ statbase/Product.asp?vlnk=10620&More=n"*

Labour Force Survey (LFS) data

The data used in this chapter are taken from the interim reweighted LFS microdata; in line with the guidance on using LFS microdata *(http://www.statistics.gov.uk/about/ Methodology_by_theme/Interim_2001-Census-adjusted_LFS_ estimates/downloads/LFS_microdata.pdf)*, rates are reported and any levels reported are consistent with the First Release, unless otherwise indicated.

The results from the 2001 Census, published in September 2002, showed that previous estimates of the total UK population were around one million too high. As a result, ONS published interim revised estimates of the population for the years 1982 to 2001, which are consistent with the 2001 Census findings. Interim national LFS estimates consistent with the latest population data have now been produced. Initial analysis work conducted by the ONS has shown that revisions to the LFS-census adjusted data have a greater impact on levels data than on rates. Generally revisions to rates are within sampling variability, while those for levels are not. This report uses adjusted data where possible, however, where adjusted data are not available only rates have been used. The most up-to-date data referred to in this chapter are for spring 2003.

SOC2000

The Standard Occupational Classification (SOC2000) was first published in 1990 and revised in 2000 to replace both the Classification of Occupations 1980 (CO80) and the Classification of Occupations and Dictionary of Occupational Titles (CODOT).

The two main classification concepts remain unchanged and are:

- Kind of work performed – job, and

- The competent performance of the tasks and duties – skill.

One of the reasons for the change in definition was the need to be in line with the International Standard Classification of Occupations.

There are nine major groups, 25 sub-major groups, 81 minor groups and 353 sub-minor groups in the classification.

The nine major groups are:

1. Managers and senior officials

2. Professional occupations

3. Associate professional and technical occupations

4. Administrative and secretarial occupations

5. Skilled trades occupations

6. Personal service occupations

7. Sales and customer service occupations

8. Process, plant and machine operatives, and

9. Elementary occupations

For further information contact:
occupation.information@ons.gov.uk

Part 4: Income

Equivalisation scales

When looking at household income, account has to be taken of the number and ages of people living in the household. This reflects the common sense notion that to enjoy a similar standard of living, a household of five adults will need a higher income than a single person living alone. The income of the household is adapted so that it can be compared with other households.

The scales conventionally take a married couple as the reference point with an equivalence value of one. A single person household has a value less than this. Children are also given an equivalisation score, depending on the number of children in the family, as is each additional adult. An overall equivalence value for each household is found by adding up the appropriate values for each person in the household. The equivalised household income is then calculated: divide the household's actual income by the household's equivalence value. Different equivalisation methods are available. The Department for Work and Pensions (DWP), the Office for National Statistics (ONS), the Institute for Fiscal Studies (IFS) and the Institute for Social and Economic Research (ISER) all use McClements equivalence scales in their analysis of the income distribution.

Quartiles, quintiles and deciles

One of the methods of analysing income distribution is to rank units (households, individuals or adults) by a given income measure, and then to divide the ranked units into groups of equal size.

Groups containing 25 per cent of units are called 'quartile groups' or quarters. Thus the 'bottom quartile group' is the 25 per cent of units with the lowest incomes. Groups containing 20 per cent of units are referred to as 'quintile groups' or

'fifths'. Decile groups – tenths – contain 10 per cent of the units.

Part 5: Living standards

Bedroom standard

The concept is used to estimate occupation density by allocating a standard number of bedrooms to each household in accordance with its age/sex/marital status composition and the relationship of the members to one another. A separate bedroom is allocated to each married or cohabiting couple, any other person aged 21 or over, each pair of adolescents aged 10 to 20 of the same sex, and each pair of children under 10. Any unpaired person aged 10–20 is paired if possible with a child under 10 of the same sex, or, if that is not possible, is given a separate bedroom, as is any unpaired child under 10. This standard is then compared with the actual number of bedrooms (including bedsitters) available for the sole use of the household, and deficiencies or excesses are tabulated. Bedrooms converted to other uses are not counted as available unless they have been denoted as bedrooms by the informants; bedrooms not actually in use are counted unless uninhabitable.

Part 6: Health

Age standardisation

Standardisation allows for comparisons across populations. Age-standardised rates are calculated by multiplying age-specific rates for the study population by the standard population structure. The European standard population is often used, as it is the closest demographic profile of England and Wales.

All cause mortality rates

All cause mortality rates are calculated by multiplying the age-specific death rates for each social class and cause of death at each point in time, by the standard population structure to give the expected number of deaths. The expected number of deaths are then divided by the number in the standard population and reported as deaths per 100,000 population. Further information on statistical methods: Bunting J (1997) Sources and Methods, in Drever F and Whitehead M eds (1997) *Health Inequalities Decennial supplement*. DS. No. 15. London. The Stationery Office pp. 236–240

Confidence intervals

Confidence intervals are a way of assessing how precisely we have measured an event of interest, such as deaths. All naturally occurring events are subject to random variability over time. For example deaths in one specific year may vary from a different year by chance alone, and the confidence interval incorporates this random variability into the measurement, resulting in a range of values for which we have a degree of confidence that the true rate value resides. The confidence level most commonly used in health related research is 95 per cent, but 90 per cent, 99 per cent and 99.9 per cent confidence intervals can also be calculated. The narrower the confidence interval the more precise the rate estimate is and vice versa.

Health Survey for England

The 1999 Health Survey focused on the health of minority ethnic groups, and included a large-scale representative sample of minority ethnic adults and children throughout the country. The sample was in two parts. One part was a boost sample designed to increase the number of informants from Black Caribbean, Indian, Pakistani, Bangladeshi, Chinese and Irish groups. (Although Black Africans were not included in the 1999 survey, development work for a future health survey among this group is being carried out.) Over 64,000 addresses were screened to establish whether there were any eligible residents from these groups. Among eligible residents at an address, up to four adults and three children were randomly selected for the survey.

The other part was a general population sample which involved selecting about 6,500 addresses. At each address, all adults and (up to two) children aged 2–15 were eligible for interview.

Household reference person (HRP)

The household reference person is defined as follows:

- In households with a *sole* householder that person is the household reference person;

- In households with *joint* householders the person with the *highest income* is taken as the household reference person;

- If both householders have exactly the same income, the *older* is taken as the household reference person.

Infant mortality by socio-economic status

In 2001, three simultaneous changes were introduced which affected reporting of infant mortality by socio-economic status. National Statistics socio-economic classification (NS-SEC) replaced social class based on occupation (see Appendix, Part 2: Socio-economic classifications); the Standard Occupational Classification was updated (see Appendix, Part 3: SOC2000); and the coding of employment status changed. The three-class version of NS-SEC ('managerial and professional', 'intermediate', and 'routine and manual') corresponds most

closely to the non-manual and manual groupings of social class. Infant mortality rates in 2000 by NS-SEC90 and NS-SEC show that differences were within 0.2 deaths per 1,000 live births in the three-class version of NS-SEC. Adjustments need to be made to NS-SEC90 (for data prior to 2001) to correct for the differences caused by the different ways NS-SEC90 and NS-SEC were derived. Comparison of actual social class against social class approximated from NS-SEC shows very little difference (within 0.1 deaths per 1,000 live births) in infant mortality rates for 'non-manual' and 'manual' groupings. Therefore it may be possible to approximate social class at this level for data from 2001.

For further information see the article entitled 'Implications on changes in the United Kingdom social and occupational classifications in 2001 on infant mortality statistics' in *Health Statistics Quarterly* 17. *http://www.statistics.gov.uk/downloads/ theme_health/HSQ17.pdf*

Life expectancy

Life expectancy at birth for a particular social class and time period is an estimate of the number of years a new born baby would survive were he or she to experience the average age-specific mortality rates of that social class and time period throughout his or her life. Life expectancy at 65 for a social class is an estimate of the number of additional years an individual would survive having reached age 65 were he or she to experience the average age-specific mortality rates of the social class for the remainder of his or her life.

Life expectancy at birth for an area in 1999 to 2001 is an estimate of the average number of years a new-born baby would survive if he or she experienced the particular area's age-specific mortality rates for 1999 to 2001 throughout his or her life. The figure reflects mortality among those living in the area in this period. It is not the number of years a baby born in the area in 1999–2001 could actually expect to live. This is both because the death rates of the area are likely to change in the future and because many of those born in the area will live elsewhere for at least some part of their lives.

7: Participation

Religion data in the 2001 Census

The Census in England and Wales asked one question about religion, "What is your religion?" The responses to this question were very similar to answers given to the Labour Force Survey question, "What is your religion, even if you are not currently practising?" – suggesting that despite slight differences in the wording, the two questions were answered on the same basis. The Census in Scotland asked two questions

about religion, "What religion, religious denomination or body do you belong to?" and "What religion, religious denomination or body were you brought up in?" The two questions produced different results, the main difference being the proportion with no religion, which was much greater on the Current Religion question. Answers given to the second question, Religion of Upbringing, were similar to those given by Labour Force Survey respondents in Scotland – again suggesting that respondents were answering on the same basis. Since the England and Wales question and the Scotland Religion of Upbringing question appear to have been answered on a similar basis, these two questions were combined to produce GB level data. The exact questions underlying all analyses were as follows:

In England and Wales: *'What is your religion?'*:

> None
> Christian (including Church of England, Catholic, Protestant and all other Christian denominations)
> Buddhist
> Hindu
> Jewish
> Muslim
> Sikh
> Any other religion (please write in)

In Scotland: *'What religion, religious denomination or body were you brought up in?'*:

> None
> Church of Scotland
> Roman Catholic
> Other Christian (please write in)
> Buddhist
> Hindu
> Jewish
> Muslim
> Sikh
> Another religion (please write in)

Northern Ireland data on religion are different to those for Great Britain because a very different Census question was asked in Northern Ireland. Respondents were asked to select which religion they considered they belonged to. Where the respondent selected 'none' they were then asked a supplementary question on which religious background they were brought up in. Some imputation was undertaken where information was incomplete. Community background figures and religion figures cannot be related to obtain information about those who stated their religion as None. When referring to the community background variable, 'None' or 'No

community background' should be used instead of 'No religion'.

The religious categories offered were all divisions of the Christian category with an 'other' religion option. Thus analysis for Northern Ireland distinguishes between Catholics and Protestants, which is not available for Great Britain.

Protestant includes 'Other Christian' and 'Christian related', and those brought up as Protestants. Catholic includes those respondents who gave their religion as Catholic or Roman Catholic, and those brought up as Catholics. The term community background refers to those belonging to and bought up in a particular religion.

Civic activities

The civic activities included signing a petition, contacting a public official working for a local council, contacting a public official working for the Greater London Assembly or the National Assembly for Wales; contacting a public official working for part of central government, contacting a local councillor, contacting a member of the greater London Assembly or the National Assembly for Wales, contacting a Member of Parliament, attending a public meeting or rally, and taking part in a public demonstration or protest.

Social activities

The fifteen common social activities included: visiting friends or family in hospital, visits to friends or family, celebrations on special occasions, visits to school, eg sports day, attending weddings and funerals, hobby or leisure activity, collect children from school, friends or family round for a meal, holiday away from home once a year, attending a place of worship, an evening out once a fortnight, coach/train fares to visit friends/ family quarterly, a meal in a restaurant/pub monthly, going to the pub once a fortnight, holidays abroad once a year.